Craft Brew

F

FRANCES
LINCOLN

Frances Lincoln Limited
74–77 White Lion Street
London N1 9PF

Craft Brew

Design: Ashleigh Bowring
Commissioning editor: Zena Alkayat

First Frances Lincoln edition 2016

A catalogue record for this book is available from
the British Library.

ISBN 978-0-7112-3845-9

Printed and bound in China

1 2 3 4 5 6 7 8 9

FRANCES
LINCOLN

EUAN FERGUSON

Craft Brew

50 homebrew recipes from the world's best craft breweries

Contents

—

Breweries

USA

Introduction

—

Why brew your own beer? After all, pubs are full of it; the shelves of bottle shops groan under the weight of all those lovely stouts, pale ales and lagers. Can you really make it better than a professional? The answer to that is: maybe, maybe not, but it doesn't really matter. Brewing your own beer is fun, satisfying and creative.

The life-affirming qualities of fermented grain have been known to humans since at least 9000BC, and today it's the world's most popular alcoholic beverage. There's been a lot of excited talk about a 'renaissance' or 'revolution' in beer, which might seem odd, given that it never went away. But it's the way we think about beer that's changing: its versatility, taste, strength, potential, even its place in society. At the heart of this is what's come to be known as craft beer.

What is craft beer?

'Craft'. Does that word in front actually mean anything? Some people say craft brewers have a small output. Well, compared to a brand like Budweiser, perhaps they do. But Lagunitas, for instance, produced 600,000 barrels of beer in 2014 at its California site. Other people think craft brewers are all independent. For the most part, that's true: craft beer lovers will tell you that a brew free of the taint of big money tastes much sweeter. Others claim that craft beer has in-your-face flavours and cancel-tomorrow ABVs, and is full of ingredients that don't belong anywhere near beer, like foraged herbs or grapefruit or tonka beans. But try Marble's Manchester Bitter (p173), a modern interpretation of an old, old style, which sits down beside you for a gentle cuddle rather than whacking you over the head: things become

less clear-cut. So let's make our own definition – craft beer is about values over volume, it's about spirit over finance, it's about soul over cynicism. If that sounds like the sort of thing you like, then craft beer is for you.

And this book will help you not only become a craft beer drinker but a craft beer brewer. Homebrewing is an integral part of the craft beer revolution – most commercial craft brewers started making it at home and there's still a close connection between them, their product and the people who drink it.

The world's best breweries

All the recipes here come direct from the world's most exciting, groundbreaking, fearless and uncompromising breweries. Take inspiration: having a go at Mikkeller's Cream Ale or Gigantic's Ginormous imperial IPA is much more enticing than making plain old generic versions. Start with something simple and move on when you feel like you're getting to grips with the techniques and you understand your equipment. And when you get more confident, use the recipes as springboards to dive off into your own creations – more/fewer/different hops at different stages, a touch of roasted malt or rye or oatmeal, complementary ingredients like fruit, herbs, spices, tea, chocolate, vanilla, coffee… You're only limited by your imagination.

Kit, extract and all-grain

Anyone can buy kits that contain
everything to make beer. (Well, a
sort-of beer.) Open a packet of mixed
malt-and-hop extract, pour it in a bucket
with some water, wait a while, drink:
more or less, that's it. But you can also
buy microwaveable meals and flatpack
furniture – it doesn't mean you should.
You may get a passable approximation
of a distant relative of beer from a kit,
but it will lack life and will provide a mere
droplet of the enjoyment that comes
from brewing from scratch. The next
progression from kit brewing is to use
dried malt extract in place of fermentable
grain: extract brewing uses a soluble
powder or syrupy substance in the
mashing stage. This can lead to decent
beer, and many homebrew journeys
begin this way. It's easier, certainly, but
will probably leave you feeling like you're
missing out on the mistakes, trials and
triumphs of real brewing. This book
recommends taking the plunge and going
all-grain from the start. You'll learn heaps
from your misses and miscalculations.
So here, all recipes are all-grain – using
real malt and real hops. It involves a bit
more work, but it's worth it.

And is 'craft' homebrewing any different from regular homebrewing? In theory, maybe not, but in principle, yes. Homebrewing as we know it today hasn't been a historically continuous practice (at least not a legal one). In Britain, for instance, homebrewing regulations insisted upon a licence until 1963; in the US, making beer at home with a higher ABV than 0.5% was illegal until 1978. Early exponents of late twentieth-century homebrewing were often attracted by financial benefits rather than creative ones, giving the practice an unenviable reputation for producing sinister buckets of undrinkable sludge (a reputation it struggled to shake off for a long time). The new generation of homebrewers find inspiration in the huge range of ingredients and beers they find within their reach.

So now, your local bottle shop or bar sells beer brewed thousands of miles away (hopefully as well as a lot brewed within walking distance). Beavertown's Smog Rocket porter, made in north London, is available in North America. Kiwis can wake up to Mikkeller's famous Beer Geek Breakfast oatmeal stout; a whole hemisphere away in Denmark, Mikkeller's online shop sells beer from New Zealand's estimable 8-Wired. Homebrew shops sell hops from all over the world, from classic English varieties like Fuggles or Bramling Cross to Australia's tropical Galaxy. You can buy malted grains of every colour – from tried-and-trusted barley to spelt, buckwheat and rye. If you're a craft beer drinker, you probably have a good idea what a saison or a witbier or a cherry sour or an imperial stout tastes like. You probably have your favourites. And now there's nothing stopping you from making your own.

Start simple, then experiment

Before you start your journey into homebrewing, remember: a recipe is just a starting point. In this book they come straight from the breweries and have been formulated and tweaked for their own processes, which are probably very different from yours. You should consider your first brew to be a test. Keep records. Also, your own equipment is just as important as ingredients; as is taking accurate measurements, hitting targets, experimenting, practising, balancing ratios and consistency.

Equipment

—

Brilliant batches of beer have been brewed for years on homemade A-Team-style collections of equipment. Don't feel like you need a full complement of steel kit before you can call yourself a homebrewer.

What you need

At its core, making beer is a simple enough process, but it's worth investing a bit of time and money getting things right.

Your kit will have a huge effect on the end product, more even than the recipe. As you become a better brewer, you'll get to know your equipment: how it behaves, what it can do, what *you* need to do to get it to achieve your targets. A fundamental understanding of the processes involved will give you a solid base to move on from. This chapter details what could be considered a minimum of what's needed to make quality craft beer at home, plus a few more bits and pieces you might consider investing in if you get serious.

Homebrewing has a history of innovating, inventing, hacking, adapting, making do, converting and ingenuity. Many bits of equipment can be adapted at home from everyday components. You can add to it as you go on. And before you splash out, consider the idea of a cooperative: open breweries, like Chaos Brew Club in Chicago, or Ubrew in London, are spaces where members can use top-grade equipment, buy ingredients and share knowledge. But it doesn't have to be so organised. A few people can pool together to install a brewing set-up in a spare room or even a shed, meaning less individual investment and more hands to join in the work (plus more mouths to drink the results). The creation of beer, much like its consumption, is better with friends.

01 Hot liquor tank

To begin a brew, you'll need to heat water to a fairly precise temperature (water when warmed becomes 'liquor' in the trade). A sizeable stovetop pan is the entry-level option. It has to be big enough to hold the total water for your brew (see 'mash' p53), to save you having to heat up twice for mash and sparge; and also if you're planning to alter the water's chemical make-up before you begin (see p28). But a purpose-built HLT with an element is more accurate and makes multi-rest infusions easier; it will also have a tap to make liquid transfer safer. Advanced models come with volume sight gauges and built-in thermometers.

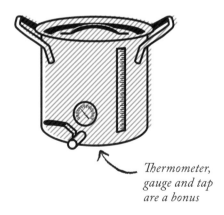

Thermometer, gauge and tap are a bonus

02 Mash tun

An insulated plastic chill box with a lid makes an inexpensive and straightforward mash tun, following the fitting of a drainage tap and some sort of filter. You can fit these yourself with basic DIY skills and basic DIY store parts – online guides abound – or you can buy them ready to use. The next step up from plastic is stainless steel. Size is important here too. The tun has to be big enough to fit your batch size; however, if it's too big the grain bed will be insufficiently deep to create effective filtering. For most of the recipes in this book, 30 litres/6 gallons capacity will work (although for the extra-high ABVs, something bigger would be helpful). A filter to separate post-mash liquid from solids is essential. These come in various forms, and all homebrewers have their favourites:

01. False bottom: a mesh that sits proud of the floor of the mash tun, with a run-off tap below it. It holds the grain but lets liquid through. This is probably the most effective homebrew method.

02. Manifold: an arrangement of copper or plastic pipes covering the bottom of the tun, with small holes to allow hydraulic drainage of the wort. This works well too, but can be harder to clean.

03. Braid: a stainless-steel weaved hose that works in a similar way to a manifold.

04. Bazooka filter: more often used in the boil kettle, but some brewers think it works just fine in a mash tun too. It's a single steel mesh tube which attaches straight to the drainage tap. Issues have been reported with sugar extract efficiency, however.

05. Bag: some brewers fill a nylon bag with their grains, which can be lifted right out after the mash.

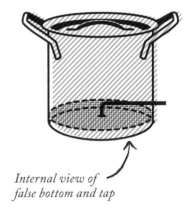

Internal view of false bottom and tap

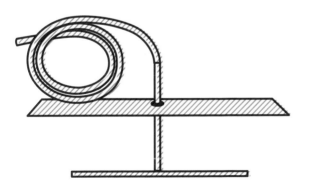

03 Rotating sparge arm

Very handy for the sparging stage, this simple bit of kit rests atop the tun and rotates when water is passed through it, showering the mash in a fine spray that won't disturb the grain bed. A cheap and easy hack is to pierce holes in a piece of aluminium foil big enough to cover the grain surface, then very slowly pour the sparging water over that with a measuring jug.

04 Boil kettle

To extract bitter flavours from hops, a vigorous boil is necessary, and household cooker hobs aren't usually powerful enough to maintain this. Boil kettles are therefore heated by an internal electric element or sit on top of a gas burner. They have to be large enough to hold the batch without boiling over – for safety's sake, for a 20 litre/5 gallon brew you'll need a 30 litre/8 gallon capacity. The shape of the kettle is important too: if the diameter is too wide, the evaporation rate will be higher than desired and too much wort will be lost. A diameter/height ratio of about 1:2 is recommended.

05 Filter

Dried hops are a beautiful thing, fragrant and flaky; boiled hops are a sludgy mess and must be kept away from the fermenter. So as with the mash tun, the boil kettle needs a filter to separate hop matter or other ingredients from the wort at the end of the boil. The options are a false bottom, a bazooka filter or a bag (although there's some suggestion that hop bags don't allow a proper extraction of oils and acids at the boil stage).

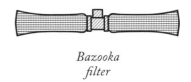

Bazooka filter

06 Wort chiller

After the boil stage, it's usually vital to cool the wort down as quickly as possible to minimise air-exposure time and chances of infection, plus it saves you hanging around. (The exception is in the case of a 'hop stand' or 'whirlpool', when hops are added to the wort after the boil and left to stand.) An immersion chiller is a coiled length of tubing which connects to cold water at one end and drains from the other; it's placed in the wort 15 minutes before the end of the boil to sanitise, and when the cold water is turned on it transfers out heat. You can make your own relatively easily from copper pipe and plastic hose.

Store-bought plate or counterflow coolers do the same thing faster and, inevitably, more expensively.

07 Airtight fermenting tub, glass jar or metal tank

A good fermentation is essential for good beer. Fermenting tubs can be made of plastic, glass (a carboy or demijohn) or steel. Plastic is cheapest, lightest and blocks out sun, but scratches relatively easily; glass allows the brewer to easily see the progress of the fermentation, but is heavy when full and can crack; steel protects the beer from sunlight and is, as ever, the most expensive.

Two such vessels allow for a secondary fermentation (see p47). They need tight-fitting lids and airlocks or blow-off tubes, and they need to be the right size to accommodate your wort plus its krausen (not a mythical sea monster, but the unappealing-looking froth that forms at this stage). A tap at the bottom makes racking easier.

08 Airlock

A bubbler airlock has water-filled chambers that keep bad stuff out of your lovely beer but let CO_2 escape: you can see fermentation taking place this way. Simple airlocks have a lid that does the same job, or a blow-off tube leads from the stopper into a small vessel of sanitised water.

09 Racking cane

Beermaking involves a lot of liquid transfer. A racking cane is attached to a siphon tube and has a sediment trap at the bottom to filter out unwanted solids when moving liquid out of the fermenter into a keg or bottling vessel. You'll need one if your fermenter doesn't have a tap at the bottom. Again, steel is pricier but more pro than plastic.

10 Bottle filler

A simple tap/tube combo that makes the final stage of brewing that bit more enjoyable. A stainless steel syphon filler allows you to fill several bottles at once.

11 Bottle capper, bottles and caps (or Grolsch-type swingcap bottles)

All that beer needs to be stored somewhere before drinking. Bottling is the usual option: you'll need caps and a capper too. Go for brown bottles to avoid the beer becoming 'lightstruck' – a term for when natural light causes a breakdown of hop acids creating a most unpleasant smell.

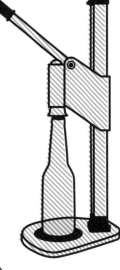

A fridge can be fitted with a thermostat

12 Heater and/ or brew fridge

Optimum fermentation occurs at fairly specific temperatures (18-20C/64-68F for ale, lower for lager), which usually have to be maintained for the duration. Too hot and the yeast will go into overdrive or die, too cold and it just won't wake up enough to do its job. Depending on environmental conditions, the wort might need to be warmed or chilled to hit these targets. Heating is easier – if you're fermenting somewhere cold, a heat pad will help maintain temperature. Chilling is harder, especially for lagering (see p113, for example). Lagering is definitely an advanced homebrew technique, but then there's not much more satisfying than a cold, crisp pilsner on a summer day. Some people use a fridge with temperature controls. A more basic option is to put the fermentation vessel in a larger tub of water, which can be iced if necessary: like the sea, it will be less susceptible to environmental temperature changes as it's a bigger body of water. Monitor temperature regularly, whichever option you choose.

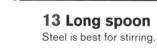

13 Long spoon

Steel is best for stirring.

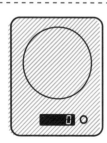

14 Digital scales

Grams and ounces matter in homebrewing. Digital is the way forward.

15 Thermometer

Some models clip on to the side of a pot, some float in liquid; some are digital, others use mercury. The more accurate yours is, the more closely you can follow recipes and control your process. Temperature is hugely important.

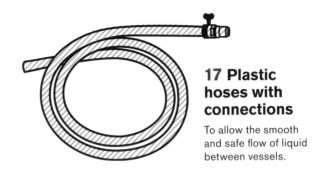

17 Plastic hoses with connections

To allow the smooth and safe flow of liquid between vessels.

16 Measuring jug

Essential for recirculation, tasting and drawing off wort.

18 pH papers or digital tester

As explained on p28, the pH of water can have an effect on the beer you make with it. Science-class strips are cheap but hard to read. A digital tester is more accurate and won't cost too much. Neither is essential for a homebrewer just starting out, but to take your brews to the next level, the chemical composition of your water has to be taken into account.

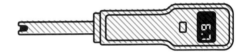

19 Hydrometer or refractometer

You probably only need one or the other, but these two bits of kit measure the specific gravity (density) of your brew at various stages (see p53). These readings help you calculate alcohol content as well as efficiency. Pure water at 20C/68F has a specific gravity of 1; wort's is higher due to suspended sugars. As a wort's sugar is converted to alcohol and CO_2 throughout the brewing process, it loses density. A hydrometer (left) is a basic instrument: it's a weighted glass thermometer-like tube with a scale, and it floats in a sample of wort in a trial jar. You can also use a refractometer, which gives readings calculated from a few drops of liquid on a prism: it's more accurate, and doesn't require temperature to be taken into account.

To use a hydrometer (which is more properly called a saccharometer, since it's measuring sugar content), firstly take a small sample of wort using the (sanitised) trial jar. Cool it down externally to around 20C/68F by immersing in cold water or swirling it around – temperature affects density (or, use a temperature conversion graph). Slowly lower the hydrometer into the wort and give it a little spin to dislodge any air bubbles. When it rests on its own, take a reading from the bottom of the meniscus at eye level.

Brew like a pro

*Advanced equipment to make
your beer even better.*

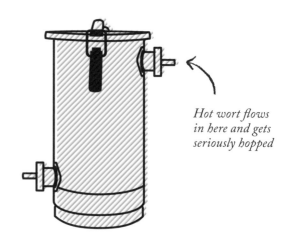

*Hot wort flows
in here and gets
seriously hopped*

01 Hopback

If you seriously get into hops and want
to add even more of that drink-me-now
aroma to your brews, consider a hopback.
It's a sealed container which fits in line
between the boil kettle and the fermenter:
it's filled with whole or plug hops, which
impart loads of flavour without losing any
of their oils to boil-off. You can make your
own – it's not too hard.

02 Wooden barrels

Chances are you've tried a barrel-aged
beer recently. Ageing ale on wood is
becoming big news as brewers look
for new and exciting roads to take their
beer down. Ex-wine, whisky, sherry,
bourbon and even tequila barrels are
used; if you've got room for a brewing
set-up, you might have room for a little
barrel too. They're sold in different sizes
and can be reused a few times for many
styles of beer. Wood chips in secondary
fermentation are sometimes employed
as a substitute.

In general, beers with higher ABVs and
rich, dark flavours age better than lighter,
fresher ones, but who's going to stop you
making that port-barrel-aged witbier if
you really want to?

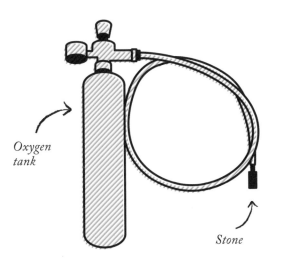

Oxygen tank

Stone

03 Aerator

At later stages of the brew, oxygen and beer are not best of pals. An exception is when racking from the kettle to the fermenter: yeast needs O^2 to live. A bit of splashing, stirring and shaking is the hands-on solution, although you can buy a tank with a ceramic or steel diffusion stone to do it more effectively. An aquarium stone with an electric pump is a thrifty hack, provided of course it hasn't spent time keeping Goldie's tank fresh.

04 Kegs, taps and CO^2

A keg-and-tap combo creates the closest legal thing to a pub in your house. Add a dartboard and you can probably start charging neighbours by the pint. Advantages of kegs: they keep beer fresh between serves, they're bigger and easier to clean and sanitise than a caseful of bottles, and they can be force carbonated (the use of a gas canister to quickly carbonate beer without having to wait for yeast to do the job in the bottle, a system employed by many craft breweries). Modern Keykegs are a plastic bag-in-barrel system that allow brewers to keg beer and dispense it using a bicycle-style handpump.

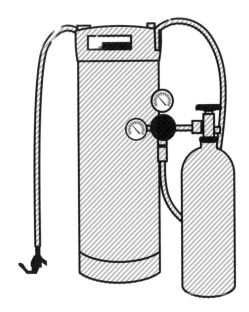

Ingredients

—

Just as you really don't need much equipment to make beer, its ingredients can be reduced to a core four: water, malt, hops and yeast. From this holy quaternity, miracles happen – every element comes in many variations, but together they form the basis of most beers.

01 Water

It might seem like the most straightforward ingredient, but even plain old H^2O needs a bit of consideration before it goes into a brew. It makes up the largest percentage of beer. Traditionally, the mineral content and pH of local water determined the types of beer that would be made in an area (London's high-carbonate water meant stouts and porters dominated, whereas the soft water in parts of Germany make an ideal base for lager). There are solutions and tablets you can add to brewing water to raise or lower the pH or hardness, but it might feel like it takes a chemistry degree to fully understand the effects of various chemicals and minerals on your ingredients. Unless your own area's water has a notably extreme chemical make-up, or you really want to recreate a particular style of beer exactly, the stuff that comes out your tap will probably be fine for your first few brews. Your water company will be able to supply a report on the compounds present in your supply if you want to get scientific, and then you can begin to tailor the water chemistry for each brew.

02 Malt

The first thing you'll probably add to brewing water is malt and other grains (collectively known as grist). Malt is a catch-all term for any type of 'malted' cereal – a grain that has gone through the process of being soaked in water to begin germination then dried in hot air to stop it. The drying is done to different degrees of intensity (heavy roasting, even). Germination allows the natural starches to be converted into sugar during the beermaking process.

Pretty much any cereal can be malted and used in beer – millet, buckwheat, spelt even – but the most-used varieties are barley, wheat, oats and rye. The intensity of the post-soak heating results in different characters – pale malt, for instance, is used as a base for many beers and doesn't add much colour; 'chocolate' malt lends deep, bitter flavours and a rich dark hue. (Roasted barley isn't malt, but is often employed in the same way, in stouts and porters.)

Malts are classified by colour in three scales – degrees Lovibond (from light 10L to 300L-plus dark malts), and the newer ERM (European Reference Method) and EBC (European Brewery Convention).

Grains need to be crushed (into about three smaller bits) before use. Brewers working towards a homemade product take on the crushing themselves using a grinder, but if you buy malt pre-crushed, try to use it straight away. It will last well in its whole form but loses potency when broken up.

Enzymes produced during germination break down long and complex grain starches into shorter lengths which can be consumed by yeast – lower temperature mashes favouring beta amylase will in general create higher alcohol but less body in the beer; mash temperatures towards the higher end of the scale favour alpha amylase, which leads to lower alcohol production and more body. A balance between both is usually favoured.

03 Hops

In a beautiful balancing act with malt, hops are the other primary flavour-creators in beer. Brewers use the (usually) dried flowers of the hop plant, which also have medicinal and antibacterial properties (before the days of scrupulous sanitation, hops had a welcome side effect of killing bacteria). They can also add a barrel-load of taste, ranging from subtle and warm to unrestrainedly floral or totally tropical, depending on the variety. Hops added at the start of the boil provide bitterness; when added throughout the process ('late hopping') they provide more powerful flavours, and at the end they create aroma in beer. Those American-style IPAs that seem to fill the room with

their ultra-fresh fruit and garden bouquet – you can guarantee a whole heap of late hops have been employed. Some hops are best for bittering, some excel at aroma, and the all-rounders do both. Hop packets list an alpha acid percentage (AA), which varies by crop and year, and to ensure consistency, brewers have to take this into account. It gives us an idea of the amount of bitterness a hop will provide. For example, the US Chinook has a relatively high AA at around 12%, whereas New Zealand's Wai-Iti brings only around 4% AA but smells like a citrus orchard in summer. Some recipes in this book list the brewers' recommended AA – if you're aiming for accuracy, you need to take this into account.

04 Yeast

Yeast is the final component in the alchemical series of reactions that end up as beer. When added to cooled wort after the hop boil, yeast sets about vigorously gobbling up the sugars in the liquid, turning them into alcohol and CO_2. Without yeast, beer would be a flat, dead and impotent liquid and the world would be a sad place. Most homebrew yeasts are of the Saccharomyces genus, although others exist, including the harder-to-handle Brettanomyces (see p57, for example). Saccharomyces comes in top-fermenting and bottom-fermenting varieties – top is more common and used for most ales; bottom needs lower temperatures to get to work and is used mainly for lagers and pilsners.

There are many varieties of commercially grown yeast, some of which add unique flavours and cope differently with the traits of the beer being brewed. Saison yeast, for instance, will introduce spicy and aromatic notes. Some yeasts are described as 'clean fermenting': they don't impart much personality but convert efficiently and quietly. Breweries often use house strains that they 'harvest' from finished brews to use in the next: this can be done at home, which is a slightly more advanced technique but ensures you have a regular supply of healthy and strong yeast.

You can buy yeast dry (to 'pitch' or add into the wort from a packet) or liquid (which may have to be fermented separately in a 'starter' along with dried malt extract and water, or wort, before pitching – see p44). Dry is convenient, easier to use and recommended for beginners, but comes in a limited range of strains. Wyeast sells 'Smack Packs', slap-activated bags of liquid yeast plus nutrients which make starters on their own; White Labs sells vials of liquid yeast that are shaken to the same aim.

Each variety of yeast has its own characteristic measurements: attenuation, which is the amount of sugar that it will convert to alcohol and carbon dioxide; flocculation, the amount it will 'clump' together into solids during the latter stages of fermentation; the optimum temperature range it prefers; and its alcohol tolerance – the level of booze it handle before it gives up. We all have that.

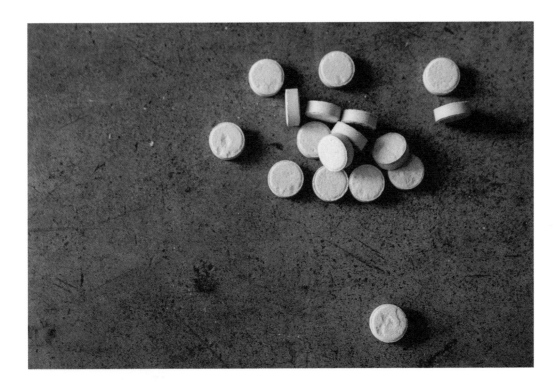

05 Other ingredients

'Adjuncts' refers mainly to unmalted grains added to a mash – corn, oats, rice – which don't take part in sugar creation but have other desirable properties: they might improve foam retention, say, or provide mouthfeel. The term can also refer to sugars – the likes of corn sugar or Belgian candi sugar – added at different stages of the brew to increase fermentation or alcohol content.

Sugar is also added to 'prime' beer just before bottling or kegging – this creates carbonation in the finished product. Light, refreshing styles – lager, amber, wheat, for instance – need more sugar than rich, comforting styles like porter or bitter.

And beer can be best pals with a huge range of other ingredients. Espresso stout, raspberry wheat beer, lemongrass saison, citrus IPA, salted porter... Those are a few uncontroversial combinations. But what about Rogue's Voodoo Doughnut, made with bacon and maple syrup? Or Two Birds' Taco Beer, a fiesta of corn, coriander and lime? Or the Popcorn Pilsner made by Indiana's Sun King brewery? There are no rules beyond what's actually drinkable – and homebrewing gives you the chance to raid the store cupboard and get creative.

Finally, many beers benefit from clarifying agents (finings). In some styles, clear beers are prized by the brewer for both visual and taste reasons, but three things can cause cloudiness: proteins (from darker grains, malted and unmalted); tannins (a grain by-product of the mash); and suspended yeast. A traditional type of clarifying agent is Irish moss (actually seaweed), added at the boil stage; it encourages the flocculation (or 'clumping') of proteins, which sink to the bottom to form sediment. Protofloc and Whirlfloc are tablet versions of finings.

Brewing your own beer

—

Brewing is a lifetime's journey, but immerse yourself in the fundamental techniques and you'll have a solid base from which to make great beer.

Sanitisation

Cleanliness, they say, is next to godliness, and in brewing it's also right beside tastiness (and safeness). Sanitisation has to come first – its importance can't be stressed enough. A whole batch of beer can be spoiled by the infiltration of unwanted bacteria or wild yeast. Warm wort is a playground for rapidly reproducing cells, and infected beer is fit only for the drain. (Unless you're Belgian – the likes of lambics are intentionally infected. But that's another story…) Every part of every piece of equipment used post-boil has to be thoroughly free of germs. Get into this habit early and you'll save yourself heartache further down the line. It's helpful to think about a 'two-steps-back' regime: sanitise anything that will touch the wort. Bottles, too, have to be thoroughly cleaned and sanitised – use a special brush or rinser.

Preparation

Most homebrewers use the power of gravity to transfer liquids between vessels in the various stages of the brew. If you have the space, a stepped podium-type arrangement will make this easier; if not, limber up for a bit of lifting and lowering. Electric inline pumps take out the struggle.

A Wyeast Smack Pack will have to be activated at least three hours before you need it. White Labs vials need to be brought to room temperature then activated 15 minutes before use. A traditional liquid yeast starter will need to be prepared 12 to 18 hours in advance. Grain should be ground as near as possible to mash-in time.

Set aside about four to five hours for a brew, longer for your first few – this is not an activity that benefits from haste. It's also not an activity that you can pause for a few hours while you go to work/sleep/the pub. And don't get too carried away with thoughts of sampling your beautiful beer any time soon. Grain to glass is about four to five weeks, when fermentation and conditioning are taken into account. It's worth the wait.

Step 1 **Mashing**

Extracting fermentable sugars from crushed grain in hot water.

01. Heat the total liquor (see 'mash' p53) in your hot liquor tank to about 10C/18F more than the recipe specifies. This could take an hour – get everything else ready, weighed and laid out while it's warming. This higher temperature allows for a bit of cooling in the tun to optimum mashing temperature, which is usually between 65C/149F and 68C/154F, although individual recipes call for variations.

02. Add the hot liquor (for volume calculation see 'mash' p53) and the well-mixed, crushed grains to the mash tun simultaneously, while carefully mixing. This can be done in half-stages, taking temperature readings to ensure it's not too hot or cold. Leave the lid off and add cold water to drop the temperature; add more hot water to raise it if necessary (record the volume of water additions, subtract from sparge).

03. Stir gently to mix everything together, distribute the water/grain and eradicate clumps. Too much vigour at this stage will drop the temperature more than desired and can lead to a 'stuck' mash, which is akin to a sloppy loaf of bread in the mash tun – just try draining wort out through that.

04. Put the lid on the mash tun. For single-rest infusions, leave for one hour (longer won't hurt). For multi-rest infusions, as a few of the recipes in this book require, it's necessary to increase the temperature during the stage to extract different malt characters. The rests are intended to develop enzymes and lead to greater efficiencies. Modern 'modified' malts, however, are designed to allow high levels of extract without multi-step infusions. This method is easier if you have a temperature-controlled mash tun; otherwise, you'll have to start off with a thicker mash (see 'mash' p53) and add hot water to hit the temperature targets. It is harder to master, certainly, and harder to keep consistent – many homebrewers deem it mostly unnecessary, some swear by it. Try it if you like to see how you get on.

05. Some brewers carry out an iodine test at the end of the mash. Take a grain-free sample of wort, put a couple of drops of common iodine in. If it turns black, there are still unfermented starches (remember that from school science?) and you should keep mashing for longer. If it stays clear/ turns slightly red, your mash is efficiently finished.

Step 2 **Lautering**

Rinsing the mashed grains of all their fermentable sugars and creating the desired pre-boil wort volume.

01. Raising the temperature of the mash to 77C/170F is known as a 'mashout'. This is done either with external heat or by adding very hot water – about 93C/200F – and serves the dual purpose of making the wort flow more freely and halting the enzyme conversion process. Some homebrewers do it; others don't bother and skip this stage without disastrous results. 'Sticky' grain bills, such as those with a lot of wheat or finely ground rye, may benefit from a mashout.

02. There are two stages of lautering – recirculation and sparging. Firstly, to recirculate (which 'sets' the grain bed), cut a piece of foil to fit the top of the grain and perforate it a few times. Draw off one or two pints of wort from the tun's tap into a jug, close the tap, and gently pour back over the foil. This is also known as 'vorlauf'. Repeat this recirculation two or three times until the runnings are free of husks and big bits of grain debris. The clearer the better.

03. There are two methods of sparging: batch and fly. This book only deals with fly sparging (see right), which is usually considered more efficient. Ensure water in the hot liquor tank is at 78C/172F, and that you have at least the volume required for the lauter (see 'mash' p53). Sparging effectively rinses the grains of all the fermentable sugars formed in the mash, creating the correct volume of rich, sweet wort.

04. A stuck mash is when grains become too thick to allow filtering of the wort and can happen with batch or fly sparging. The sign of a stuck mash is when no wort flows out the bottom, even though the tap is open and there's liquid in the tun. To fix it, close the outlet tap on the tun and give it all a little

stir; recirculate a couple of times after this as in step 2 to 'set' the bed again, and leave for 15 minutes before running off again. If this doesn't work, you might need to try other methods like a more forceful stirring or the reapplication of heat to loosen the liquid.

05. Before the wort is boiled in the kettle it can be useful to take a gravity reading at 20C/68F (see p53). This will be your pre-boil gravity.

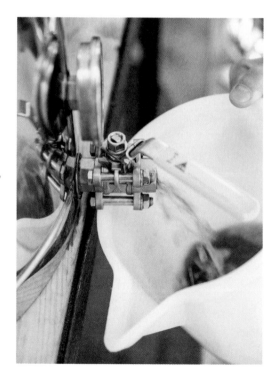

06. If you're using a sparging arm, set it up above the tun. Connect its inlet hose to the hot liquor tank, and a hose to the tap at the bottom of the tun. Lead the other end of this hose to the boil kettle.

07. Partially open the hot liquor tank tap, causing the arm to spin and water to sprinkle out; simultaneously open the tap at the bottom of the tun. The object here is to produce a continuous and steady flow of wort down through the grain bed and out. If the grains seem to 'pull away' from the walls of the tun a bit, increase the water in; if there's a layer of water above the grain bed, decrease it. Too much water weight could collapse the bed, making filtering impossible.

08. As soon as the kettle's element is fully covered in wort, you can turn it on to begin to boil – this will save time. Keep the water flowing until you've reached the desired pre-boil volume in the kettle (see 'mash' p53).

An alternative fly sparging method involves a flexible, perforated food-grade plastic hose, which sits atop the grain bed and is connected to the hot liquor tank and trickles water. Or, easier still, continue sparging with the foil method described on the previous page: refill your jug with 78C/172F water from the hot liquor tank and gently sprinkle it over the top. Repeat this several times.

Yet *another* method that homebrewers use is to spread water over the grain surface with a big metal spoon and a hose that's connected to the hot liquor tank.

Whichever way you do it, the principle and aim is the same, and it should take anything from 45 minutes for a standard grain bill up to 90 minutes for heavy mashes. Make sure you only use the right amount of sparging water as calculated at the start of your brew (see 'mash' p53).

Step 3 Boiling

Extracting bitterness, flavour and aroma from hops (and killing unwanted bacteria).

01. By now you should have the correct volume of wort in the kettle, and it should be on its way to boiling. Putting the lid on the kettle will get you there quicker.

02. Adding hops before the water even boils is known as 'first wort hops'.

03. When the wort hits a rolling boil, you're ready to commence the hop schedule. Break up any big lumps in the hops then drop each addition straight in as the recipe directs, giving it a stir each time. Leave the lid partially off throughout the boil. This allows for the escape of sulphur compounds (which give beer an unwanted 'cooked corn' flavour), or chlorine, should your tap water contain it; it also lets you see if the liquid is in danger of boiling over. You will lose some wort to evaporation (see 'mash' p53), but you should have allowed for this.

Your first couple of boils will give you a clear idea of exact measurements. If you're using finings of any sort, like Whirlfloc (see p33), this is the stage you'll add them (usually ten or 15 minutes from the end).

04. Keep the water bubbling merrily for the duration. If you're using a coiled immersion cooler and not performing a hop stand, insert it (without water flowing) 15 minutes before the end to sanitise.

05. At the end of the boil, remove the heat source (brewers call this flameout) and add any final hop additions (ie for a hop stand or whirlpool).

06. Take a small sample and use a hydrometer or refractometer to take a gravity reading (OG).

Step 4
Hop stand

Giving hops a long, lazy bath in warm wort for maximum aroma.

Conventional wisdom claims that the wort needs to be cooled as quickly as possible after the boil. However, as some of the recipes in this book indicate, a hop stand can add huge aromas to the final beer and many homebrewers now incorporate it. Basically, it simply involves adding a load of aroma hops and leaving them in contact with the cooling wort for anything between ten and 45 minutes. This is also known as 'whirlpool hops', due to the pro technique of spinning the wort, creating centrifugal force to form a pyramid of solids in the middle of the kettle, allowing for easier drainage. You can do this if you wish, but a hop stand can still be performed without a whirlpool. If your recipe doesn't call for a hop stand, skip to Step 5 on the following page.

Step 5 **Cooling & aerating**

Dropping the wort temperature and preparing it for the introduction of yeast.

Whether you've performed a hop stand or not, it's imperative the wort is now cooled as quickly as possible to minimise risk of infection (and for two other reasons: to get it to the yeast-friendly temperature indicated on the packet and to minimise hanging-around time. A batch of wort can take hours to cool naturally). See p20 for the different chillers you can use (or simply dunk the whole kettle in a big bath of iced water, which takes a long time and only works for non-electric stovetop pots, of course). From now on, anything that comes into contact with the wort must be considered a potential risk to the health of your beer. Sanitise. Also, at this stage it's a good idea to think about yeast – if it needs to be rehydrated, start it while your wort is cooling.

Immersion cooler

If you're using an immersion cooler, connect hoses to the ends – one for cold water in, one out. Turn on the cold water tap as high as it safely will go and ensure the output leads to a drain or sink. Stir the wort with a sterilised spoon to ensure maximum cooling efficiency.

Take regular measurements until the wort temperature is within the range specified on the yeast packet. Turn off the cold water input and remove the chiller.

Transfer into the fermenter will have to be carried out now – either with gravity or a siphon. Splashing is desirable at this stage – oxygen in the wort is essential for the yeast to start fermenting.

Plate cooler

Connect hoses to the correct inputs and outputs. You'll be extracting the wort as it chills – so you'll have to balance the output carefully to ensure that the liquid flowing directly into the fermenter is at the right temperature (around 20C/68F or less). If it's too high, close off the tap at the bottom of the boil kettle a little. Splashing at this stage is to be encouraged – oxygen in the wort is essential for the yeast to begin fermenting. Keep this going until you've drained the boil kettle into the fermenter.

In the fermenter

01. Depending on your efficiency and evaporation, the volume of wort at this stage may vary. If you have more or less than the intended batch size, the chances are that your gravity will be a bit off target – the beer will still be eminently drinkable, just not exactly the ABV you were aiming for.

02. Take another gravity reading. This will be your original gravity (OG), vital in determining final ABV. Compare it to the target OG in the recipe (see p53).

03. Give the wort a stir to avoid any hot spots, then take a temperature reading. If it's too hot, the yeast you're about to pitch will not work or could even die off, and you'll have to pitch another batch. Which you may or may not have hanging around somewhere. It's a good idea to have a spare.

04. Aerate the wort. Like us, yeast can't live on beer alone – it needs oxygen. (Don't aerate wort above 26C/80F – it can cause oxidation, which is not the same as aeration and makes your beer taste weird.) Homebrew shops sell aeration equipment; the simple way of aerating is to put the fermenter lid on tight and shake it all for a few minutes.

Step 6 **Pitching yeast**

There's a party going on in your fermenting vessel. The sugars are sitting guarding the booze stash and the hops have got boring old water up on the dancefloor. But it's not going off just yet. Pitching the yeast is like chucking John Belushi in and locking the door: things are going to get wild.

How much yeast should you use? One packet per 20L/5 gallon batch will probably be enough for beers up to 11% ABV or so. For higher-gravity beers, it's advisable to use two packs or make a starter culture. As mentioned on p32, there are two forms of commercial yeast, dry and liquid. Liquid yeasts should be stored in the fridge until use, although it's best not to keep them for too long (anything more than a few months will render them sluggish and feeble). Dry yeast is much hardier. A third kind, wild yeast, is floating all around you right now – it would get involved with your beer if you gave it the

chance, but the outcome would be unpredictable to say the least. Stick to the store-bought stuff at first; spontaneous fermentation is for the confident only.

Some manufacturers of dry homebrew yeast recommend rehydrating dry yeast before pitching. They'll tell you that the rehydration process has the potential to damage yeast cell walls, and so should be carried out on a smaller scale at a certain temperature before pitching. Some homebrewers disregard this advice and sprinkle the yeast straight on top of the wort, which is most of the

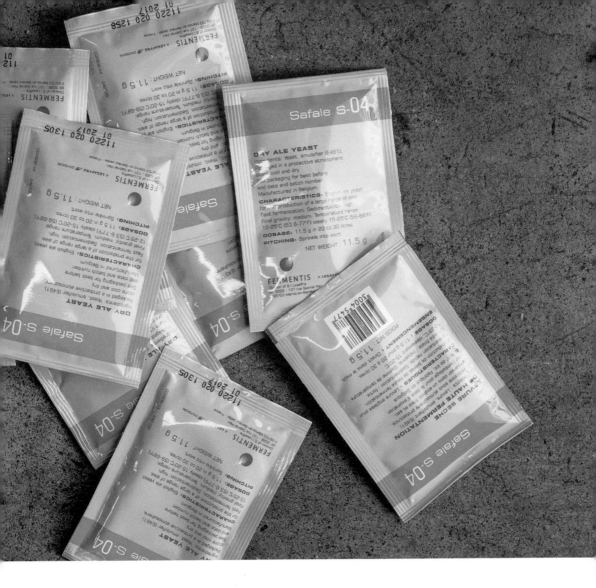

time absolutely fine, but not guaranteed to work. Best follow the instructions on the packet (and always sanitise the outside of the packet too before opening). If the packet doesn't have instructions (where did you find this stuff?), do it like this: boil four times the amount of water as you have yeast. Allow to cool to around body temperature (hopefully 37C/98F) in a sanitised jar. Sprinkle room-temperature yeast over and leave for 15 minutes. Stir it in gently, and after another 15 minutes, check first that the yeast temperature is within 10C/18F of the wort it's going into, then send it in. Liquid yeast, provided the nutrient pouch (if there was one) was activated three hours before and it's at the correct temperature, can be poured right in too.

When you've pitched the yeast, wave goodbye to the wort and shut the lid or seal the top. Next time you open it, you'll have beer. Put the airlock in the hole (with a bit of sanitised water, if it's the bubbler type).

Step 7 **Fermenting (and dry-hopping)**

Good beer demands a good fermentation. Give the yeast what it needs and it's hard to fail.

In some ways, fermenting is the easiest step in brewing, because it involves passing over all the work to the yeast: but fermenting is also perhaps the most important. Give the yeast a hand by ensuring the fermentation vessel is stored in a dark place at the temperature indicated in the recipe. Primary fermentation should begin within 12 hours of pitching: the evidence will be activity in the airlock as lots of CO_2 is produced. (If nothing happens after 24 hours, the yeast has probably not worked. Don't despair: pitch your spare packet, making sure you follow the condition instructions carefully.) If you have a glass vessel you'll be able to see the scummy-looking krausen forming on the top of the wort, but if you're fermenting in steel or plastic, don't be tempted to open the lid to have a look. That's asking for infection.

Under normal conditions, this phase could last up to ten days for ales – it's hard to be accurate, because yeast is free and alive and doesn't follow instructions. Keep monitoring it – when the activity from the airlock has slowed right down, it's time to either rack off into a secondary fermenter (not strictly essential for a homebrewer, most of the time) or simply leave for longer to condition. The yeast is still working, albeit at a slower pace, and the beer is clearing. Three weeks is about the maximum you'd want to leave it on the yeast cake without racking off.

When you're satisfied the phase is over (and satisfaction comes with experience), it's time to take a gravity reading. This will be your target final gravity (FG), and will be used to determine ABV (see p52).

If you're making lager, it's time for the lagering phase – another fermentation stage at a lower temperature.

Some brewers then practise 'cold crashing' on lagers or beers, chilling the beer to between 1C/33F and 5C/40F for between a couple of days and a week to aid in clarifying.

If you're dry-hopping, as many of the recipes in this book suggest, after primary is the time to do it. How long should you dry-hop for? As with most aspects of homebrewing, there's no straight answer. Three to five days is a good bet, but experiment with less or more if you like. The hops need to be in contact with the wort long enough to give up their oils. Your choice of fermentation vessel will affect the method you use: some people dry hop using a muslin bag, to avoid extra matter in the wort, but that becomes hard to physically fit into a plastic or glass carboy. So hop plugs are handy at this stage because they're just more practical. If you're not racking and filtering out to a bottling vessel (see Step 8), a bag is pretty much essential to avoid hop lumps in your beer.

Step 8 Priming, bottling & conditioning

The last few stages before the best one (drinking) involve setting the stage for carbonation and giving the beer somewhere peaceful to rest.

You're so close to having real beer. The liquid in the fermenter is no longer wort: it's malty, hoppy and alcoholic, but flat and underdeveloped. For fizz, it needs priming with sugar, usually brewing sugar (a simple glucose which adds no flavour and is easily converted to CO_2 by the yeast). Mix up a solution according to the volumes of carbonation required: brewing software makes this a cinch. You can rack the beer out into another vessel before bottling, to minimise sediment transfer into bottles: if you do this, put the sugar solution in then rack on to it. Or just use the fermenting vessel and be careful. Pour the solution into the almost-beer, stirring very gently but ensuring it's well mixed. Attach the scrupulously sanitised bottling tap to the vessel and fill the scrupulously sanitised bottles. To suffer contamination at this stage would be like breaking your ankle on the last 100 yards of a marathon. Using a capper, fix the sanitised caps on solidly. Put the bottles somewhere dark and cool for two weeks, although you'll find that another one or two on top often helps. (Some beers, like Nøgne Ø's barleywine on p162, need longer to mature.)

And as for the next stage, you probably don't need any guidance. Get a couple cold, say cheers, and drink the best beer you'll ever taste. Until the next batch.

How to follow these recipes

—

Beer recipes come with their own code, one of gravities, yields, times, weights and percentages. Once you understand how they correspond to what you actually have to do at home, they're simple (and you can start writing your own!).

All beer recipes are created with efficiencies and equipment in mind – the same ingredients could lead to different results on different sets. So consider your first brew a test. Keep records. Equipment is just as important as ingredients, as is taking accurate measurements, hitting targets, experimenting, practising and consistency. The recipes in this book were created by pro brewers; if you can't recreate a particular mash schedule or fermentation profile, adapt, but keep the principles intact!

When laid out in steps, homebrewing seems simple enough. But delve a bit deeper into the science and it can become a bewildering mass of figures, percentages, weights and measures. Like most hobbies, you can get as geeky as you like. Don't be alarmed: dive in, figuratively speaking, and before long a beautiful calm will descend over your brewing. The relationships between ingredients and their properties will be revealed. Efficiency and consistency will move within reach. Your equipment will become an extension of you and you'll be at one with the malt, hops and yeast.

Or, at least, you'll get the hang of it. Either way, great beer is the result. There are good homebrew calculators online and in app form, but to get to grips with the science underpinning the art will lead to better beer. You only need a basic understanding of maths to brew, and if you don't have that, are you sure you're even old enough to be drinking beer?

ABV target

Alcohol by volume. This is a pretty vital figure – will you end up with a breakfast beer, or one you need to clear space in your diary to drink? ABV is a target, not a guaranteed figure, though. To calculate it, you'll need OG and FG readings (see p53), which are also targets. A simple homebrew formula is:

$$ABV = (OG - FG) \times 131.25$$

Use specific gravities with a point (ie 1.054). The relationship between gravity and ABV is not linear, so this formula is never going to be completely spot-on, especially at higher ABVs. Use software or an online calculator for increased accuracy.

Yield

All the recipes in this book are to a homebrew batch size of 20L/5 gall. That's the amount you're aiming to get into the fermenter, although even after that, some liquid may be absorbed by yeast, dry hopping, dead space etc. Water, malt, hops and yeast can be scaled up or down effectively to make more or less beer, should you want to. The yield figure is also a target – if it's higher or lower, your gravity and ABV might be awry.

OG and FG targets (original gravity and final gravity)

The two most significant targets in a homebrew recipe are original and final gravity. Not only do they allow us to calculate ABV, but they're an indication of how efficient a brew was, and also, the FG will tell us when fermentation is finished. When brewers talk of 'brewhouse efficiency', they're referring to the ability to which their system can extract potential fermentable sugars of the grains from start to finish. Due to differing ingredients, efficiency can't be considered uniform across brews. All the recipes in this book assume a 75% efficiency, which is not a bad target. As you become a better brewer you'll want to take efficiencies into account and measure your own. A good software like Beersmith is invaluable.

Grain

All recipes in this book suggest grain weights as well as percentages. Basically, if you don't want to concern yourself too much yet with efficiencies, use the weights; if you have a clear idea of how your equipment performs and what efficiency you can hit, use the ratios and the results will be more accurate.

Mash

Mashing is, simply put, grain plus water. Mash water is split into two volumes – strike water and sparge water – and you'll have to know how much to use of each. To calculate strike water we firstly calculate mash thickness, ie the ratio of water to grain. A standard ratio is 2.6L of water to 1kg of grist (1.25 quarts to 1lb). To then calculate the sparge water, we have to allow for losses to, among other things, grain absorption, trub absorption (see p183), hops absorption (boil and dry), all vessel dead space and boil evaporation. You'll only really know how much your system is likely to lose after a bit of trial

and error. (Boiling water for an hour in your kettle, volume measured before and after, will reveal your evaporation rate.) You can assume that 1kg of malt holds on to 1L of water (roughly 1lb/1 pint). So to work out total liquor, add lost volume on to target yield; to get the sparging volume, simply subtract the mash volume from this total. As a guideline, you'll probably need to be putting around an extra 7L/1.5 gall above final yield into the boil kettle.

Hops

Some breweries in this book specify alpha acid percentages in their recipes. Alpha acids are compounds extracted from hops in the boil which provide bitterness in beer. Bitterness is measured in International Bitterness Units (IBUs). AA and IBU are related: more AA leads to higher IBU; a greater weight of hops or a longer boil time also leads to a higher IBU. Alpha acids in hop varieties vary from crop to crop, so to achieve exact IBUs, hop weights will need to be adjusted.

If you need to adjust a hop weight to your own packet AA%, get your calculator out. Here's a formula:

Original AA% x original hop weight / AA% of new hop = weight of new hop

And as with grain, you might not always be able to get the hop variety specified in a recipe, especially in times of agricultural shortage. Alternatives abound.

Yeast

Many breweries use a house strain: the recipes here suggest commercial strains and, again, you can find substitutes in case of unavailability. Choose something similar.

Fermentation

Stick to this temperature as closely as possible till FG is reached and fermentation has finished.

Carbonation

Introduce the correct weight of priming sugar to give the finished beer the correct amount of fizz. This varies according to temperature, volume and style of beer, so it's always easiest to use an online calculator.

Wheat, saison & sour

Wheat, weizen, wit: when malted it makes beer smooth and refreshing; unmalted wheat is sharper. Saison is a light and sparkling Franco-Belgian farmhouse ale that takes on added flavours perfectly, while sours use different yeasts and bacteria to result in a recognisable tart taste.

Bruery Terreux

Orange County, California, USA

BERET

RASPBERRY IMPERIAL SOUR WITBIER

---

20 L / 5 GAL | ABV 9%
OG **1.076** | FG **1.010**

There's a group of craft beer lovers who don't just buy it and drink the stuff. They buy it, cellar it, trade it, age it and show it off (then hopefully drink it too). In the world of rare beer collecting, one brewery's name comes up again and again: The Bruery (this Terreux side brand was created for sours in 2015). There's emphatically no IPA – founder Patrick Rue's team specialise in barrel-aged, sour, experimental, rested-on-fruit styles, plus revivals and completely original creations. Many of these beers blossom after a long dark rest on wood; Beret, however, can be fermented on steel (or a neutral wine barrel, or a demijohn/carboy) and enjoyed fresh (although it too will pick up complexity over time). The base is a smooth Belgian wit with minimal hopping, but the Lacto bacteria and Brett yeast take it to a new level. The Brett will get stuck into any malt sugars left over (and sugar from the raspberries), all the while producing its trademark spicy, fruity, farmy flavours. Brewer Andrew Bell recommends using sturdy bottles capable of withstanding a lot of CO_2 (you should aim to carb to around 2.75 volumes).

GRAIN
Weyermann pilsner malt, 3.4kg/7lbs 8oz (60%)

Great Western unmalted wheat, 2.27kg/5lbs (40%)

MASH
67C/152F for 60 mins

HOPS
(60 minute boil)

German Magnum 15.2% AA, 6g/0.21oz, first wort hops

YEAST
White Labs WLP400 Belgian Wit Ale or Wyeast 3944 Belgian Witbier

Your favourite Lactobacillus brevis (12 days into fermentation)

Your favourite Brettanomyces bruxellensis, 1,000,000 cells per ml (12 days into fermentation)

FERMENT
18C/65F, then allow to free rise; full fermentation and souring will take around 2 months

OTHER INGREDIENTS
Crushed coriander, 12g/0.4oz, boil for 10 mins

Bitter orange peel, 12g/0.4oz, boil for 10 mins

Yeast nutrient and Whirlfloc, boil for 10 mins

Raspberry purée, 726g/1lb 9.6oz, or whole raspberries, 826g/13.1oz, 12 days into primary

Brooklyn Brewery

Brooklyn, New York, USA

The story of the Brooklyn Brewery is so fascinating it deserves its own book. Luckily it has one. Beer School: Bottling Success at the Brooklyn Brewery is full of anecdotes and details, facts and figures, history and legend behind the Williamsburg enterprise, which is still as cool as a freshly cracked cold one after almost 30 years on the scene. Brooklyn is truly craft beer royalty: it was founded in 1988 by an ex-Middle East correspondent and keen homebrewer (Steve Hindy) and a banker (Tom Potter), and the unquestionably iconic emblem was created by

Milton Glaser, designer of the I ♥ NY logo. Since 1994 the output has been under the stewardship of brewmaster Garrett Oliver, who's become something of an authority in the world of craft brewing. Brooklyn has built a reputation with its non-traditional advertising and its no-compromise beers, including the the harmoniously balanced East IPA, the made-for-outdoor-drinking Summer Ale and the world-famous Brooklyn Lager, which has been surprising, intriguing and converting major-label beer drinkers since 1988 with its Vienna-style malty richness.

Brooklyn Brewery

Brooklyn, New York, USA

SORACHI ACE
US-HOPPED SAISON

▬

20 L / 5 GAL | ABV **7.2%**
OG **1.062** | FG **1.008**

A relatively recent addition to the Brooklyn gang is Sorachi Ace, a classic Belgian farmhouse ale with a New York accent. Traditionally, saisons were made for hardworking agricultural workers in the countryside of the Wallonia region, with a fairly tight selection of ingredients – European malts and grains, low-alpha acid noble hops – but they're great fun to brew because they can cosy up with all sorts of other hops and flavourings. This twenty-first-century reimagining uses only one hop, the Northwestern-by-way-of-Japan Sorachi Ace, which provides a flowery, lemony character you won't get anywhere else. And the technique in this recipe is great evidence of the way that staggered deployment throughout the boil can draw out a real range of flavours, from bitterness through flavour to aroma. An essential element of saison is Belgian yeast, which makes its presence known through fruity, spicy, ester notes. The result is straw-coloured, refreshingly carbonated, food-friendly and supremely thirst quenching – ploughing fields will be a breeze after a couple of these.

- -

GRAIN
Pilsner malt, 5kg/11lbs (92%)

MASH
50C/122F for 10 mins, 63C/145F for 60 mins, 67C/152F for 15 mins, mash out at 75C/168F. Draw off wort at 1.054 SG and add corn sugar

HOPS
Sorachi Ace 12% AA, 14g/0.5oz, 60 mins

Sorachi Ace 12% AA, 14g/0.5oz, 30 mins

Sorachi Ace, 56g/2oz, 0 mins

Sorachi Ace, 84g/3oz, dry hop 5-7 days

YEAST
Wyeast 1214 Belgian Ale or White Labs 500 Trappist Ale

FERMENT
22C/71F

OTHER INGREDIENTS
450g/1lb corn sugar (8%)

8 Wired Brewing

Warkworth, New Zealand

SAISON SAUVIN
NZ-HOPPED SAISON

━━━━

20 L / 5 GAL | ABV **7%**
OG **1.055** | FG **1.002**

In New Zealand, they say anything can be done with a bit of No 8 wire. It was a gauge used for fencing, and came to symbolise the classic Kiwi DIY attitude: adaptability and resourcefulness and just-bloody-get-on-with-it. It seems you can even make good beer with No 8 wire – Søren Eriksen has won awards including NZ Champion Brewery in 2011. Compare this saison, which stars the one-of-a-kind Kiwi hop Nelson Sauvin, to Brooklyn's Sorachi Ace on p60, or Burning Sky's Saison à la Provision on p68, and you'll see the huge variations in malt, hops, yeast, additions and techniques that exist in the style. Some advice from Søren: "The higher finishing fermentation temperature is important for proper attenuation. You can use many kinds of yeasts, but it's important to get the extreme level of attenuation that we get from the 3711. So if you use a lower attenuator, include up to 10% dextrose in the fermentables. Plus, a small amount of dry-hopping with Nelson Sauvin doesn't hurt, but we don't do it…" There is no substitute for Nelson Sauvin either – this beer won't be the same without it.

GRAIN
Pilsner malt, 2.71kg/5lbs 15.6oz (59%)

Pale ale malt,1.06kg/2lbs 5.4oz (23%)

Wheat malt, 370g/13oz (8%)

Caramalt, 180g/6.3oz (4%)

Flaked wheat, 180g/6.3oz (4%)

Acid malt, 90g/3.2oz (2%)

MASH
Mash at very low temperature to get the required attenuation, 64C/147F (or lower if you are comfortable with it), for 60 mins

HOPS
(60 minute boil)

Nelson Sauvin, 42g/1.5oz, first wort hops

Nelson Sauvin, 84g/3oz, whirlpool

Motueka, 42g/1.5oz, whirlpool

YEAST
Wyeast 3711 French Saison

FERMENT
Start fermentation at 21C/70F, then let it rise to 27C/81F or so over the course of 4–5 days

Three Boys Brewery

Christchurch, New Zealand

THREE BOYS WHEAT
BELGIAN-STYLE WIT

▬▬▬

20 L / 5 GAL | ABV 5%
OG 1.050 | FG 1.012

New Zealand is a small country with a widescreen outlook. This is especially true in the country's craft brewing industry, which punches well above its weight in both hemispheres. Three Boys' Ralph Bungard is president of the Brewers' Guild of NZ and an ex-scientist – the methodical and enquiring mind is a useful one to have in a practice like brewing, and Ralph's won a heap of awards for his consistently top-class beers (especially the Oyster Stout, made with some of the world's best bivalves from Bluff on New Zealand's South Island). Three

Boys is a deliberately small-scale brewery focused on quality rather than global domination, and like all of its brews, this Wheat is true to its roots, being a classic Belgian style with prominent yeast characteristics, a cloud-like head, coriander and citrus. But NZ brewers always leave their own mark on their beers, and here it's through a fully native hop bill (including the fresh and tropical Motueka) and the unique Meyer lemon zest. Wheat in a mash tun can get sticky, so bear that in mind when lautering – you can use rice hulls to keep it loose.

- -

GRAIN
Gladfield NZ Light Lager malt, 2.01kg/4lbs 6.9oz (47%)

Gladfield NZ Wheat Malt, 1.34kg/2lbs 15.3oz (32%)

Gladfield NZ Raw Wheat 670g/1lb 7.6oz (16%)

Gladfield Gladiator Pale Crystal 10L 300g/10.6oz (5%)

MASH
69C/156F for 60 mins

HOPS
Green Bullet 13.9% AA, 7.5g/0.26oz, 90 mins

Motueka 7.5% AA, 3.5g/ 0.1oz, 10 mins

Motueka 7.5% AA,10g/ 0.35oz, 0 mins

YEAST
Wyeast 3994 Belgian Wit

FERMENT
20C/68F

OTHER INGREDIENTS
Fresh Meyer lemon zest, 22g/ 0.8oz, boil for 5 mins

Ground coriander, 33g/ 1.2oz, boil for 5 mins

three boys

Wheat

Three Boys Wheat evokes ancient abbey ales, when yeasts ~~~~~~~
~~~~~~ instead of hops were added for bitterness. We use ~~~~~~~
~~~~~ that with the wheat malt produces the authentic frothy ~~~~~
cloudiness and huge flavours sought in this wit bier (white ~~~~~~~~
The addition of coriander and citrus zest really make this beer ~~~~~

Brew By Numbers

Bermondsey, London, England

01|01 CITRA SAISON
HOPPY SAISON

▬▬▬

20 L / 5 GAL | ABV **5.5%**
OG **1.044** | FG **1.002**

You've probably realised by now that brewing does involve a lot of numbers, but it means something different here. This innovative London brewery was set up in 2011 by two keen homebrewers, Tom Hutchings and Dave Seymour, who from the very start wanted to do things properly. A trip to the Low Countries opened their eyes to the vast range of idiosyncratic beers produced there, and back in Britain they set about making their own with Belgian rigour and attention to detail, but unlimited imagination. The 'numbers' in the name refers to a unique cataloguing system: the first part denotes style (08 is stout, 14 is tripel, for instance) and the second is the recipe: 05|08 is a Mosaic IPA. And here's where it all started, with Citra Saison. Traditional saisons definitely don't involve Washington hops, but as with Brooklyn's Sorachi Ace (see p60) and 8 Wired's Saison Sauvin (see p63), the style warms to them perfectly. The greengrocer's-basket bouquet of lychee, grapefruit and melon from the Citra is perfect in this light, smooth and sparkling saison.

GRAIN
Low-colour Maris Otter pale malt, 1.35kg/2lbs 15.6oz (36.5%)

Pilsner malt, 1.08kg/2lbs 6.1oz (29%)

Wheat malt, 810g/1lb 12oz (22%)

Flaked wheat, 270g/9.5oz (7.5%)

MASH
65C/149F for 60 mins

HOPS
Hallertauer Magnum 12.9% AA, 5g/0.15oz, 60 mins

Citra 12% AA, 10g/0.35oz, 10 mins

Citra 12% AA, 10g/0.35oz, 5 mins

Citra 12% AA, 50g/1.8oz, flameout. Steep for 10 mins before chilling

YEAST
Wyeast 3711 French Saison, or other saison yeast of your choice

FERMENT
24C/75F, ideally hold for 48 hours then allow to free rise, ideally maintain at 27C/80F

OTHER INGREDIENTS
Dextrose, 180g/6.3oz (5%), added slowly as the wort is coming to a boil to ensure it dissolves and doesn't scorch

Cracked coriander seeds, 10g/0.35oz, boil for 5 mins

Burning Sky Artisan Brewers and Blenders

Firle, Sussex, England

SAISON À LA PROVISION
SAISON

20 L / 5 GAL | ABV **6.5%**
OG **1.052** | FG **1.002**

The British Guild of Beer Writers brewer of the year 2014 Mark Tranter was a founder of Dark Star (see p140). It still makes great beer, but he's transferred his passion elsewhere. Mark set up Burning Sky in 2013 as, literally, a long-term project: its main focus is wood-aged, vatted beer; he uses yeasts that take their time to make a product that's in no hurry to mature. Think of it as slow brewing. Saisons are a particular favourite of Mark's, and this Saison à la Provision is a labour of love. "We have French oak foudres that were built for us and are only used for this beer," he says. "We transfer into them after one week of primary fermentation and age the beer for three months. The 'wild yeasts' are becoming resident in the wood; consequently the beer is constantly developing, batch to batch. For homebrewers, unless you have a wine barrel, try ageing the beer on lightly toasted French oak chips or spirals. Our saison yeast strain, plus the Brett/ Lacto, are not commercially available as vials, they were harvested from various sources. For the Brett, choose a gentle variety."

GRAIN
Pilsner malt, 3.9kg/8lbs 9.6oz (85%)

Wheat malt, 220g/7.8oz (5%)

Spelt malt, 220g/7.8oz (5%)

Cara Gold, 220g/7.8oz (5%)

MASH
65C/149F for 60 mins

HOPS
East Kent Goldings 3.75% AA, 25g/0.9oz, 75 mins

East Kent Goldings 3.75% AA, 12g/0.4oz, 15 mins

Saaz, 23g/0.8oz, 0 mins

Celeia, 23g/0.8oz, 0 mins

Sorachi Ace, 25g/0.9oz, 0 mins

YEAST
A saison strain: primary fermentation

Brettanomyces: pitch when SG is 1.015

Lactobacillus: pitch when SG is 1.015

FERMENT
Start at 22C/71F and let rise to 25C/77F for a cleaner, less phenolic beer

Lagunitas Brewing Company

Petaluma, California, USA

LITTLE SUMPIN' SUMPIN'
PALE WHEAT ALE

▬

20 L / **5** GAL | ABV **7.5%**
OG **1.070** | FG **1.016**

Sonoma County is a pretty laidback place. It's got mountains and streams, stunning Pacific beaches, famously mellow residents and that sunny California climate. Lagunitas Brewing Company, founded in 1993, has its home there and used to hold informal taproom get-togethers at precisely 4.20pm every Thursday afternoon. If you understand the significance of that time, you're probably as mellow as a Sonoman yourself. Lagunitas is now a major US brewing operation, but its beers are still perfect to kick back with: its IPA is an unparalleled example of the type of West Coast beer that started the craft revolution all those years ago. This Little Sumpin' Sumpin' has a large proportion of wheat, giving it a silky-smooth mouthfeel – and an explosion of piney, aromatic hops means it smells just as good as it tastes. Avoid a stuck sparge while brewing it by mashing thinly and keeping the liquid flowing freely. Lagunitas filters Little Sumpin' Sumpin', which you can do yourself for a clearer glassful – homebrew stores sell the equipment you'll need. This beer's one for the hopheads (or heads of any sort).

- -

GRAIN
2-row American pale malt, 3.23kg/7 lbs 1.9oz (50%)

American wheat malt, 2.46kg/ 5 lbs 6.8oz (38%)

English torrified wheat, 720g/ 1lb 9.4oz (11%)

German toasted (roasted) wheat malt, 80g/2.8oz (1%)

MASH
65.5C/150F for 60 mins, mashout at 75C/168F

HOPS
Nugget pellet 9% AA, 9g/0.3oz, 90 min

Horizon pellet 12.5% AA, 1.5g/0.05oz, 90 min

Summit pellet 17.5% AA, 1.5g/0.05oz, 90 min

Willamette pellet 5.2% AA, 7g/0.2oz, 45 min

Santiam pellet 5.6% AA, 23g/0.8oz, 15 min

Willamette pellet 5.2% AA, 8g/0.3oz, 15 min

Cascade, Centennial and Simcoe pellets, 20g/0.7oz of each, dry hop

Chinook pellet, 24g/0.85oz, dry hop

Columbus pellet, 13g/0.4oz, dry hop

Amarillo pellet, 15g/0.5oz, dry hop

YEAST
White Labs WLP002 English Ale

FERMENT
17–18C/62–65F for 36 hours, then to 20C/68F for 36 hours, then 21C/70F to end

OTHER INGREDIENTS
Add gypsum if you're in a particularly low-mineral water area

Freigeist

Cologne, Germany

KÖPENICKIADE
BERLINER WEISSE

▬

20 L / 5 GAL | ABV 3.5%
OG 1.037 | FG 1.010

Brewing in Germany has a uniquely regulated history. The medieval Reinheitsgebot purity laws are not enforced now, but the industry remains regionalised: salty gose is brewed in Leipzig, altbier in the Lower Rhine. Braustelle, however, is an innovative little brewery in Cologne that makes beers with reverence for the past and a forward-looking attitude; from its experimental offshoot Freigeist ('free spirit') comes this modern take on a Berliner weisse. These increasingly popular beers are sour (from the Lacto bacteria), refreshing (low alcohol, light malts) and easy on hops. This version replaces the traditional wheat with spelt malt, a gluten-free grain which adds a slight nuttiness. The techniques here are fairly advanced. Make a starter with the Lacto before pitching. Wort pH should be less than 4.5 to ensure optimum conditions for its development. You'll need to maintain a high temperature while it ferments, too. Wort splitting is not a traditional method, but it makes the results more predictable (and still taste great). The style responds positively to fruity additions, and it also ages well in bottle.

GRAIN
Pilsner malt, 1.52kg/3lbs 5.6oz (50%)

Spelt malt, 1.1kg/2lbs 6.8oz (36%)

Carapils, 430g/15.2oz (14%)

MASH
63C/145F for 30 mins, then 72C/162F for 30 mins, then mash out at 78C/172F

HOPS
Saphir, 10g/0.35oz, 60 mins

Saphir, 10g/0.35oz, 0 mins

YEAST
Fermentis K97 German Wheat, and White Labs WLP677 Lactobacillus

FERMENT
Split the boiled wort into two separate fermentation tanks. Pitch Fermentis K97 into one (at 20C/68F), and the Lactobacillus into the other (35C/95F). After primary fermentation, rack both into a secondary fermentation tank. Leave at 20C/68F for 10 days. Condition at 4C/39F for 14 days

Baladin

Farigliano, Piedmont, Italy

OPEN WHITE
BIERE BLANCHE

▬

20 L / **5** GAL | ABV **5%**
OG **1.051** | FG **1.016**

You'd be hard pressed to find anywhere in the world that takes food and drink more seriously than Italy: it seems that every Italian understands the importance of the land and what's produced on it. Think of Baladin as being part of the beer arm of the Slow Food movement. Local cherries, pears, orange blossom, pumpkins and heather honey are used in founder Teo Musso's brews, which often come in magnum sizes for proper dinner-table sharing. He's big on cooperation and collaboration too, hence the Open series of 'crowd sourced' beers. This is where Open White comes in: Baladin's version of a biere blanche uses malted wheat as well as the raw wheat traditional in a Belgian biere blanche, and it's dry-hopped too. The orange and coriander, however, bring things back closer to Brussels, and note the use of gentian, a distinctively bitter root which predates hops as a historical beer flavouring. Don't use finings in this recipe – suspended yeast and cloudiness is an important aspect of the white beer style, plus it should be well carbonated for a big fluffy head, which the wheat helps maintain.

GRAIN
Pilsner malt, 4.17kg/9lbs 3.1oz (87%)

Wheat, 440g/15.5oz (9%)

German weizen malt, 180g/6.3oz (4%)

MASH
Mash in at 50C/122F; then 48C/118F for 20 mins; 62C/143F for 40 mins; 69C/156F for 20 mins; mash out at 78C/172F

HOPS
Perle 8% AA, 2g/0.07oz, 90 mins

Perle 8% AA, 3g/0.1oz, 45 mins

Mittelfrüh 5% AA, 8g/0.3oz, 45 mins

Perle 8% AA, 3g/0.1oz, 0 mins

Amarillo 8% AA, 12g/0.45oz, dry hop

YEAST
Wyeast 3942 Belgian Wheat

FERMENT
20C/68F, then rack off the yeast and add the dry hops and second lot of spices. Reduce the temperature to 4C/39F for 15–20 days before bottling

OTHER INGREDIENTS
Sweet orange zest, 2g/0.07oz; bitter orange zest, 2g/0.07oz; crushed coriander, 22g/0.77oz, to be added at the end of the boil. Stand for 30 minutes

Crushed coriander, 4g/0.14oz; gentian root, 1g/0.03oz, added with dry hops at the end of fermentation

Crooked Stave Artisan Beer Project

Denver, Colorado, USA

ORIGINS
BURGUNDY SOUR ALE

20 L / 5 GAL | ABV **6.5%**
OG **1.053** | FG **1.006**

As the craft beer world begins to appreciate the power of sour, one name is at the vanguard of this modern expedition into classic Belgian and French styles. Chad Yakobson founded Crooked Stave in 2010 after years of studying the science of fermentation (read his dissertations online for unsurpassed insight). Few brewers have such a knowledge of the mysterious Brettanomyces yeast and its wild relatives, and his beers are sought-after and revered. They're sometimes challenging but always sophisticated, brewed with respect for tradition and a constant desire to progress. This is Chad's recipe for his twist on the classic Flanders red. Stick to a low-profile, low-AA hop like Hallertau or one of its New World relatives (Mt Hood, say) – bitterness is to be avoided. Skill and time is needed from primary fermentation onwards. Flanders reds get their unique sour/fruity/winey notes from long ageing on oak (although you can use glass with oak chips). Then, batches are typically blended to balance extreme flavours and maximise complexity – a process that gets easier with experience!

GRAIN
2-row pale malt, 1.65kg/3lbs 10oz (35%)

Vienna malt, 1.65kg/3lbs 10oz (35%)

Carahell, 660g/1lb 7.3oz (14%)

Caramunich I, 330g/11.6oz (7%)

Special B malt, 330g/11.6oz (7%)

Carafa Special II (dehusked), 90g/3.2oz (2%)

MASH
Mash in at 65C/149F. Rest for 30 mins. Recirculate for 10 mins. Mash out at 75-76C/167-169F for 10 mins

HOPS
(90 minute boil)

6% AA hop, 11g/0.4oz, first wort hops

6% AA hop, 11g/0.4oz, 30 mins

YEAST
For primary fermentation, something clean. Then add a mixed culture of Brettanomyces and Lactobacillus bacteria

FERMENT
For a clean primary fermentation, follow standard ale temperatures. After this, age on oak at 17-19C/ 63-66F for 12-18 months. Particularly long rests in barrel may require more yeast before bottling (something powerful but clean)

Red, amber & rye

Caramel malt gives beer a rich, auburn tone and warm, toasty flavours. Rye in small amounts is recognisably earthy and spicy, and is increasingly given a starring role in craft beers. Amber falls between lager and ale, with conspicuous malt and middling alcohol levels.

Anchor Brewing

San Francisco, California, USA

ANCHOR STEAM BEER
STEAM BEER/CALIFORNIA COMMON

▬

20 L / 5 GAL | ABV 4.5%
OG 1.050 | FG 1.016

The story of Anchor Brewing is the story of American craft beer. It was established in California by a German brewmaster in 1896, back when *all* brewing was craft brewing – there was no other way. Prohibition curtailed Anchor's activities from 1920, and the nationwide shift towards macro-produced lagers threatened its existence in the late 1950s, but blessedly it's still here and more popular than ever. Anchor makes several great beers at its loveably old-fashioned San Francisco brewery, many of them in the pioneering spirit of its founders (Liberty Ale was the blueprint for the US IPA that the world can't get enough of these days; the California Lager is faithful to a nineteenth-century pioneer's standard). The beer that made the Anchor name – Steam – is a 1970s revival of the traditional California Common style, which was practically extinct at that time. Nowadays it's venerated, with its own yeast strains and a hop blend that's tailor-made for its profile (US Northern Brewer, with a minty, piney character). Anchor Steam Beer is pure liquid history.

GRAIN
*2-row pale malt, 4.1kg/
9lbs 0.6oz (87%)*

*Crystal 40L malt, 600g/
1lbs 5oz (13%)*

MASH
65C/149F for 60 mins

HOPS
*US Northern Brewer pellets
9.6% AA, 14g/0.5oz, 60 mins*

*US Northern Brewer pellets
9.6% AA, 7g/0.25oz, 20 mins*

*US Northern Brewer pellets,
9.6% AA, 14g/0.5oz, 0 mins*

YEAST
*White Labs WLP810 San Francisco
Lager or Wyeast 2112 California
Lager*

FERMENT
*16C/61F for 7 days then
19C/66F for 3 days. Store cold
for approximately 2 weeks before
serving*

Saint Arnold Brewing Company

Houston, TX, USA

BLUE ICON
RYE IPA

---

20 L / 5 GAL | ABV **7.8%**
OG **1.067** | FG **1.013**

Another homebrewer-turned-pro (there are many in this book), Brock Wagner was an investment banker by trade when he founded Saint Arnold in 1994; it's now Texas's oldest craft brewery but its new releases are still anticipated with fervour, especially those that are part of the limited Icon range. Brock brought a business mind to beermaking, taking his start-up statewide then across the Deep South into Florida. However, without good beer, a good business plan is just numbers on a page, and you can hang your hat on the fact that Saint Arnold makes good beer. This one's from that Icon series, and uses two types of rye – Weyermann rye malt and the darker, richer CaraRye – for a rounded spicy flavour. It's not all about the rye though – Briess Victory is a biscuit malt, very lightly toasted, which adds a 'baking bread' flavour without too much colour. The big hop additions (especially the Mosaic at the end) gives a real West Coast character to this beer. Note that it's dry hopped twice – once warm then once in the cold crash stage for even more hop oil retention.

GRAIN
Rahr 2-row pale malt, 5.44kg/ 12 lbs (79%)

Weyermann rye malt, 900g/ 2lbs (13%)

Weyermann CaraRye, 340g/ 12oz (5%)

Briess Carapils, 114g/4oz (1.5%)

Briess Victory, 114g/4oz (1.5%)

MASH
67C/152F for 60 mins

HOPS
(60 minute boil)

Columbus 16.3% AA, 34g/ 1.2oz, first wort hops

Simcoe 13% AA, 8.5g/0.3oz, 15 mins

Chinook 10.5% AA, 6g/0.2oz, 15 mins

Chinook 10.5% AA, 21g/0.75oz, 0 mins

Cascade 6.5% AA, 21g/0.75oz, 0 mins

Mosaic 11.5% AA, 64g/2.25oz, warm dry hop within 2 or 3 SG points of FG

Mosaic 11.5% AA, 14g/0.5oz, cold dry hop 5 days before packaging

YEAST
White Labs WLP007 Dry English Ale

FERMENT
21C/70F, cold crash at 0C/31F for 7 days prior to packaging

Brewfist

Lombardy, Italy

CATERPILLAR
AMERICAN PALE ALE WITH RYE

—

20 L / 5 GAL | ABV 5.8%
OG 1.055 | FG 1.011

Along with Baladin (see p74) and Del Ducato (see p168), Brewfist is proof that Italy deserves its place at the top table of European craft brewers. Brewfist is less immediately Italian than those two: the name suggests something a bit commanding, and indeed it concentrates on US-style ales (like the Spaceman IPA or the X-Ray imperial porter), plus collaborations with craft beer luminaries like Prairie and To Øl. One such hook-up (with Denmark's Beer Here) resulted in this Alice in Wonderland-inspired recipe, and it's a winning combination: punchy malts and a decent whack of hops from the resinous US Columbus and the tropical-citrus Kiwi Motueka. This is a great example of the way that rye, even in small amounts, can add its own personality to a brew: 10% will supply a gentle, earthy, spicy dryness, but in bigger proportions it becomes more assertive. Advice from a caterpillar: this is a great beer to try as one of your first brews, with just two hop varieties used cleverly through the boil, and enough complexity to keep things interesting.

- -

GRAIN
Pale ale malt, 3.96kg/ 11.7oz (80%)

Rye malt, 500g/1lb 1.6oz (10%)

Caramalt, 300g/10.6oz (6%)

Crystal malt 10L, 100g/ 3.5oz (2%)

Wheat malt, 100g/3.5oz (2%)

MASH
66C/150F for 45 mins, 78C/ 172F for 5 mins

HOPS
30g/1.06oz Motueka, 10 mins

8g/0.28oz Columbus, 10 mins

30g/1.06oz Motueka, whirlpool

8g/0.28oz Columbus, whirlpool

30g/1.06oz Motueka, dry hop

15g/0.53oz Columbus, dry hop

YEAST
Danstar Nottingham Ale

FERMENT
20C/68F

Two Birds Brewing

Spotswood, Victoria, Australia

———

Maybe because of beer's unfortunate former reputation as a bloke's drink, the perception still exists that brewing is a bloke's business. It's not true: all over the world, women are tending their mashes and boils, and the open-mindedness of the craft beer world hopefully breaks down any old-fashioned barriers to entry, for both drinkers and makers. What's still a bit more rare though is a completely female-founded and operated brewery. Jayne Lewis and Danielle Allen set up Two Birds in 2011 after an eye-opening trip to the craft beer heartland of the USA's West Coast, and in 2014 opened The Nest, a dedicated brewery and tasting room in Spotswood, a suburb of Melbourne in Australia. But when you taste their beers, you'll realise that it's not important whether it was made by Aussie birds or Aussie blokes –

it's just great. The brewery's success is built on a core range that includes the flagship Golden Ale, Sunset amber ale (see the next page for the recipe) and Taco Beer, made with wheat, corn, lime and coriander, and every bit as enticing as it sounds. At the brewery tap you might find the more leftfield likes of a rhubarb saison or red ale with vanilla and cacao, but what's experimentation without consistency? It's not the barrel-aged spiced tripel that's going to win over that 99% who don't yet drink craft beer. And after a hard day at work, you're probably not going to reach for that 120-IBU IIPA. Two Birds don't make beer for beer nerds, they make beer for everyone. To do that and win awards and see year-on-year expansion is arguably harder than continually making boundary-breaking beers.

Two Birds Brewing

Spotswood, Victoria, Australia

SUNSET ALE
RED ALE

———

20 L / 5 GAL | ABV **4.6%**
OG **1.048** | FG **1.014**

Sunset Ale is Jayne and Danielle's second-ever creation as Two Birds. It's an American-style red or amber ale (the difference between the two isn't worth getting worked up about), but 'sunset' sums up the colour far better – it would delight a shepherd, that's for sure. It has won stacks of awards in Australia for its rich, biscuity caramel flavour (from the Munich and amber malts) and citrussy combination of US and local hops. Amber/red ales are designed to have a fuller body and more involving maltiness than pale ales, but are still thirst-quenching and balanced – along with the summer ale style, they're perfect for hot Aussie weather. The handful of wheat in the grain bill ensures the head on the Sunset Ale sticks around to the last drop, while the Citra/Cascade/Galaxy trio at the end of the boil makes for a seriously zesty finish. One of the Two Birds, Jayne Lewis, was previously head brewer at Mountain Goat (see p95), and along with their Hightail, Sunset represents all the best things about Australian session ales.

- -

GRAIN
Traditional ale malt, 2.71kg/ 5lbs 15.6oz (63%)

Munich malt, 640g/1lb 6.6oz (15%)

Pale crystal malt, 340g/12oz (8%)

Amber malt, 210g/7.1oz (5%)

Wheat malt, 210g/7.1oz (5%)

Dark crystal malt, 80g/2.8oz (2%)

Roasted malt, 80g/2.8oz (2%)

MASH
67-68C/152F-154F for 40 mins

HOPS
Centennial, 2g/0.07oz, 60 mins

Citra, 7g/0.2oz, 20 mins

Cascade, 7g/0.2oz, 20 mins

Galaxy, 7g/0.2oz, 20 mins

Citra, 5g/0.15oz, end of whirlpool

Cascade, 5g/0.17oz, end of whirlpool

Galaxy, 5g/0.17oz, end of whirlpool

Citra, 13g/0.4oz, dry hop

Cascade, 13g/0.4oz, dry hop

Galaxy, 13g, 0.4oz, dry hop

YEAST
Fermentis US-05 American Ale

FERMENT
18C/65F

Brú

Trim, County Meath, Ireland

RUA
IRISH RED ALE

—

20 L / 5 GAL | ABV **4.2%**
OG **1.044** | FG **1.011**

This brewery's name is pronounced as you'd imagine: by fortunate coincidence it comes from the Gaelic Brú na Bóinne, a prehistoric site of burial north of Dublin in County Meath. In a country with a young but flourishing craft beer industry, Brú keeps one eye on tradition and another on the world at large – look out for its take on the world-beating Irish dry stout (Dubh, meaning black) and this red ale. Irish red ale is a unique style similar to Scottish ales (creamier than most English bitters), gentle enough to enjoy a few pints, with a deep coppery hue from the combination of pale and dark crystal malts. Standard Irish red ales have modest hop bills, but Brú's Rua uses the fruity and flowery tones of the classic US Cascade for a modern twist: maybe it's not by the book, but that's what craft brewing's all about. The brewers recommend four teaspoons of Irish moss (see p33 and p182) with ten minutes to go in the boil to keep the beer bright, and add: "Fermenting at 25C/77F creates a lot of ester formation which brings the hop aroma up and enhances the flavour."

GRAIN
Irish pale ale malt, 3.47kg/7lbs 10oz (86%)

Crystal 150L malt, 280g/ 9.9oz (7%)

Torrified wheat, 280g/ 9.9oz (7%)

MASH
70C/158F for 60 mins

HOPS
Magnum, 27g/0.95oz, 60 mins

Cascade, 20g/0.7oz, 10 mins

Cascade, 20g/0.7oz, 0 mins

YEAST
Danstar Nottingham Ale or White Labs WLP039 Nottingham Ale

FERMENT
25C/77F

Lervig Aktiebryggerie

Stavanger, Norway

RYE IPA
RYE IPA

—

20 L / 5 GAL | ABV **8.5%**
OG **1.076** | FG **1.013**

Mike Murphy is one of the best-travelled brewers in Europe. First off, he's from Pennsylvania, where the alcohol laws are among the meanest in the US. After starting out as a homebrewer, he worked professionally in Italy and Denmark (including brewing for Mikkeller) before ending up in southwestern Norway as brewmaster of Lervig, now one of the country's biggest and best. In a typically internationalist Scandinavian style, he's collaborated with tons of other breweries (see p154 for Lervig and Põhjala's imperial porter) and is now busy keeping Norway on the international craft beer map with beers that range from the Carlsberg-besting Pilsner to Lucky Jack APA and this Rye IPA. It's just about strong enough to be considered a double IPA, but the high alcohol is there to stand up to the hop bitterness and the uniquely flavoured rye. Rye can be used up to percentages of even more than 50 in some grain bills, but here, with just under 20, it makes its dry spiciness subtly but firmly known. Some people grind rye malt separately from the rest of the grist to get a finer grain size.

- -

GRAIN
Pilsner malt, 4.93kg/10lbs 13.9oz (74%)

Rye malt, 1.27kg/2lbs 12.8oz (19%)

Oats, 200g/7oz (3%)

Crystal malt 10L, 130g/ 4.6oz (2%)

Crystal malt 150L, 130g/ 4.6oz (2%)

MASH
Mash in at 61C/142F, rest at 68C/154F for 45 mins, mash out at 78C/172F

HOPS
A good bittering hop to 65 IBU, ie 65g/2.3oz of 10% AA hop, 60 mins

Centennial, 24g/0.8oz, 30 mins

Chinook, 29g/1oz, 15 mins

Citra, 29g/1oz, 10 mins

Simcoe, 29g/1oz, 0 mins

Simcoe, Citra, Centennial, 29g/ 1oz of each, dry hop

YEAST
An American ale strain

FERMENT
20C/68F

Mountain Goat Beer

Richmond, Victoria, Australia

HIGHTAIL ALE
BRITISH-INSPIRED PALE ALE

▬

20 L / 5 GAL | ABV **4.5%**
OG **1.043** | FG **1.009**

The Aussies have a habit of taking English inventions and effortlessly improving them. Cricket's a prime example, or you could have rugby, and here's another: Mountain Goat's Hightail Ale. The Victoria brewery took the classic British bitter and gave it a full Shane Warne-esque spin, retaining the traditional warm malt and all-important balance that makes the style such a fine session sipper, but adding a heap of floral New World hops (Pride of Ringwood is a quintessential early-addition hop Down Under). It's full-bodied too (from the crystal malt blend and the small portion of wheat). As one of Australia's earliest new-wave craft breweries (founded in 1997), Mountain Goat has had a long time to perfect Hightail and its other laidback beers like the New World Summer Ale or the Fancy Pants Amber ale. If you're ever in inner Melbourne, stop by the Goat Bar in Richmond to try the whole range (plus limited 'Rare Breed' editions) on tap. A final tip from Goat brewer Dave: "Carbonate gently and drink fresh!" Hightail, by the way, is perfect for watching cricket with.

GRAIN
Pale malt, 2.55kg/6lbs 6.3oz (69%)

Munich malt, 510g/1lb 2oz (14%)

Medium crystal malt, 240g/ 8.5oz (8.5%)

Wheat malt, 200g/7oz (5.5%)

Dark crystal malt, 80g/2.8oz (2%)

Roasted malt, 30g/1.1oz (1%)

MASH
67.5C/153.5F for 30 mins

HOPS
Pride of Ringwood, 20g/0.7oz, 60 mins

Cascade, 50g/1.76oz, 0 mins

Galaxy, 10g/0.35oz, 0 mins

YEAST
Wyeast 1056 American Ale

FERMENT
21C/70F

Pale ale, IPA & lager

—

Pale ales are balanced and very drinkable with fragrant hops. IPAs are more hop-heavy (usually with dry hops, originally to keep them from spoiling on long sea journeys) and stronger. Lager is clear and refreshing, and mostly made with bottom-fermenting yeast.

Evil Twin

Brooklyn, New York, USA

BIKINI BEER
AMERICAN IPA

———

20 L / **5** GAL | ABV **2.7%**
OG **1.026** | FG **1.006**

The twin in the name of this pioneering Danish gypsy brewer is Jeppe Jarnit-Bjergsø; the other half of the pair is Mikkel Borg Bjergsø, founder of pioneering Danish gypsy brewer Mikkeller (see p108). There's an ocean between them now, as Jeppe plans all his adventurously brewed beers out of Brooklyn, New York (his phenomenally productive output includes The Talented Mr Orangutan orange stout, and Ryan And The Gosling pale ale). This Bikini Beer is not so much a breakfast beer as a bedside table beer – but its fairly innocent 2.7% ABV hides a huge hop hit, much of it from Falconer's Flight, an expansively aromatic Pacific Northwest pellet blend containing Simcoe, Citra and Sorachi Ace among several others. Bikini Beer is the sort of summery brew you could drink all day. And we could all learn a lot from Jeppe's thoughts on making beer. "My idea of brewing is pretty simple," he said in a 2011 interview. "I don't care too much about the process, about what yeast or if I do it the right way. The only thing I care about is the result." Important advice whether you're on your first brew or your thousandth.

- -

GRAIN
Canadian pilsner malt, 1.75kg/3 lbs 13.7oz (66%)

Thomas Fawcett pale crystal malt 27L, 300g/10.6oz (11%)

Weyermann Carafoam, 250g/8.8oz (10%)

Weyermann or Best Munich malt 10L, 250g 8.8oz (10%)

Flaked oats, 75g/2.6oz (3%)

MASH
67C/153F for 20 mins, 69C/156F for 20 mins, mashout 76C/169F

HOPS
Simcoe 13% AA, 23g/0.8oz, 60 mins

Simcoe, 10g/0.35oz, 15 mins

Cascade, 10g/0.35oz, 15 mins

Falconer's Flight pellets, 20g/ 0.7oz, 5 mins

Falconer's Flight pellets, 10g/0.35oz, 1 minute

Falconer's Flight pellets, 34g/ 1.2oz, dry hop

Simcoe, 17g/0.6oz, dry hop

YEAST
Wyeast 1056 American Ale

FERMENT
21C/70F

EVILTWIN
BREWING

BIKINI
BEER

12 FL OZ.
INDIA PALE ALE

Gigantic Brewing Co

Portland, Oregon, USA

—

There's one problem with being a brilliant professional brewer. You make a brilliant beer, and everyone loves it. So you make more. Everyone drinks all that, so you make more. And more. And more… Before you know it, you're brewing the same beer over and over again. This is maybe the reason why brilliant craft brewers love to experiment, pushing the boundaries of what can be called beer. But in Portland, Oregon, a couple of time-served brewers have come up with a solution. Make a few beers, sell them till they run out, then make some different ones. A surefire remedy for brewhouse boredom. It takes confidence to say, "Sure the last beer tasted good, but this one's going to taste even better." And it takes even more confidence to then put the recipe for last week's beer on the website so everyone can share the Gigantic largesse.

After collective decades in the industry, founders Ben Love and Van Havig wanted to get back to basics, opening the manageably compact Gigantic to allow them both to concentrate on the fun part: brewing beer. Their #3 was The End of Reason, a strong, dark Belgian-style ale. And #24, Pipewrench, was an old-tom-gin barrel-aged IPA. Bang On, #16, was an English pale ale. And not only is the beer in the bottles unique every time, the label artwork is too. Gigantic is official beer sponsor of Portland's Design Museum, so you'd expect it to look amazing – and every release is realised by a different artist. This is certainly not the most cost-effective way to label a beer. But it's definitely the coolest.

Gigantic Brewing Co

Portland, Oregon, USA

GINORMOUS
IMPERIAL IPA

---

20 L / 5 GAL | ABV **8.8%**
OG **1.078** | FG **1.012**

This Ginormous American imperial IPA is one of Gigantic's year-round brews. It lives up to its name – this beer is all about the hops, and it brings it with seven assertive varieties all jostling for attention. This is probably not a recipe to try for your first ever brew. There's a lot of malt in weight terms, but it's not really meant to be balanced in flavour. The sugar is there to bump up the ABV and make sure the sweetness of the malt doesn't get in the way – IIPAs are dry. This heavy grain is going to need careful attention. And with so much dry-hopping, you're going to lose a fair bit of wort to absorption. Ben from Gigantic makes an important point about end-of-boil IBUs too: "Note the very low hop weights at the beginning and heavy weights at the end. Large, high-alpha additions at the end of boil give a lot of IBUs – especially if you leave the hops for 45 minutes post-boil before cooling." A 45-minute hop-stand? Ben's a pro – pay attention. Don't skimp on the yeast either. To be on the safe side you can use extra (maybe another half packet) and consider making a starter.

GRAIN
Great Western Northwest Pale Ale malt, 5.7kg /12lbs 9oz (89%)

Weyermann Munich malt I, 270g/9.5oz (4%)

MASH
65C/149F for 60 mins

HOPS
Magnum, 12g/0.4oz, 90 mins

Cascade, 80g/2.8oz, 15 mins

Cascade, 55g/1.9oz, 0 mins

Crystal, Mosaic, Simcoe, 30g/1.1oz of each, 0 mins; rest for 45 mins before cooling

Cascade, 40g/1.4oz, dry hop 1 (1 day after reaching FG)

Citra, 20g/0.7oz, dry hop 1

Simcoe, 20g/0.7oz, dry hop 1

Cascade, 40g/1.4ozoz, dry hop 2 (2 days after dry hop 1)

Citra, 20g/0.7oz, dry hop 2

Simcoe, 20g/0.7oz, dry hop 2

YEAST
Wyeast 1728 Scottish Ale

FERMENT
20C/68F

OTHER INGREDIENTS
Raw sugar, 480g/0.9oz (7%), added to the boil

Thornbridge Brewery

Bakewell, Derbyshire, England

KIPLING

SOUTH PACIFIC PALE ALE

▬

20 L / 5 GAL | ABV **5.2%**
OG **1.050** | FG **1.011–1.012**

The pretty little Peak District town of Bakewell, right in the middle of England, is famous for two things: the Bakewell pudding (a delicious jam and custard tart), and the incredible beers made by Thornbridge. From humble roots in the grounds of the stately Thornbridge Hall to today's globally exporting state-of-the-art operation, via winning shedloads of awards along the way, the brewery has won fans with beers of just about every style. Kipling is a pale ale with a short list of ingredients: don't make the mistake of thinking it's simple,

however. With one malt and only two hops, there's no place to hide; good brewing technique is essential to match the Maris Otter pale malt with the grape-and-gooseberry flavours of the famous NZ Nelson Sauvin hop. To get the bitterness balanced perfectly with the Sauvin, Thornbridge brewmaster Rob Lovatt has a tip: "Keep the Nelson Sauvin constant and alter bittering to achieve 40-45 EBU." (EBU is European Bittering Units: apart from some slight molecular differences, it's more or less the same as IBU.)

- -

GRAIN
Maris Otter pale ale malt, 4.65kg/10lbs 4oz (100%)

MASH
67-69C/152-156F for 60 mins

HOPS
Magnum, 17g/0.6oz, 60 mins

Nelson Sauvin, 50g/1.8oz, in the hopback

YEAST
White Labs WLP001 California Ale

FERMENT
20C/68F

Boneyard Beer

Bend, Oregon, USA

NOTORIOUS
TRIPLE IPA

———

20 L / 5 GAL | ABV 11.5%
OG 1.100 | FG 1.012

A boneyard is a lot where retired aeroplanes, cars, bikes, engines – any sort of metal machinery – goes to be stripped down and reappropriated. It's an apt term for Tony Lawrence's Oregon brewery, opened in 2010 with two co-founders. With a healthy brewing history on his CV (including time at Deschutes, see p150), Tony started making his own beer in downtown Bend with bits of kit collected from all over north America. It was upgraded when he moved to bigger premises, but the magpie spirit remains. Oregon and the Pacific northwest is true hops country, and this raved-about triple IPA gives them a platform to shout loud from: Boneyard hops harder than a one-legged trampolinist. Such perfection in a glass is not easily obtained, as the massive malt bill (including flaked barley) will result in a stuck mash if you don't sparge very carefully, plus the bucketfuls of Citra and Mosaic will mean you'll lose a fair bit of wort from dry-hopping (although the hop oil saves a bit there). Give the yeast a fighting chance too – "pitch very heavy and oxygenate massively!" says Tony.

- -

GRAIN
Pale malt, 6.77kg/14lbs 14.8oz (80.5%)

Munich malt, 250g/8.8oz (3%)

Flaked barley, 250g/8.8oz (3%)

Acidulated malt, 120g/4.2oz (1.5%)

MASH
64–65.5C/148–150F for 60 mins

HOPS
Fuggles, 13g/0.45oz, mash hop

CO² alpha hop oil, 1.5g/0.05oz, 60 mins

Citra, 5g/0.15oz, 20 mins

Mosaic, 5g/0.15oz, 20 mins

Citra, 5g/0.15oz, 10 mins

Mosaic, 5g/0.15oz, 10 mins

CO² alpha hop oil, 1.5g/0.05oz, 5 mins

Citra, 5g/0.15oz, 0 mins

Mosaic, 5g/0.15oz, 0 mins

Citra, 25g/10.9oz, whirlpool

Mosaic, 25g/10.9oz, whirlpool

Citra and Mosiac, 20g/0.7oz of each, dry hop 1 (pull out yeast first)

Citra and Mosaic, 53g/1.9oz each, dry hop 2 (2 days later, after dry hop 1)

YEAST
Wyeast 1968 London ESB Ale, 2 packs

FERMENT
Start at 20C/68F and allow to rise 0.5C/1F every 24 hours to 23C/73F, if you can

OTHER INGREDIENTS
Dextrose, 980g/2lbs 2.6oz (12%), boil for 30 mins

Mikkeller

Copenhagen, Denmark

——

If somebody was to survey a cross-section of worldwide brewers on their most respected peer, one name might come out on top: Mikkel Borg Bjergsø, a Danish former school teacher who founded Mikkeller in Copenhagen with a friend in 2006. Following the pioneering principles of US microbrewers, Mikkel took an internationalist outlook and practically drew up a blueprint for the current stage of the global craft beer revolution. First off, Mikkeller has made literally hundreds of different bold, innovative beers with resolutely top-class ingredients, from the plain great Stateside American IPA to a oak-barrel-aged spontaneously fermented blueberry sour. Mikkeller's more straightforward beers are just brilliant versions of their type, but the experimental brews are pure imagination in a bottle – they're challenges that demand to be taken up and drunk, but are always enjoyed. Mikkel was more or less the first ever 'gypsy' brewer, having no premises

but instead designing recipes to be realised remotely. He has a laidback attitude to brewing that emphasises fun, creativity and the social aspect of beer over science and exclusivity. He collaborates constantly with likeminded brewers in Australia, Europe and the US. He puts instantly recognisable artwork on his labels, which is clearly created with as much love as the beer itself (drawn by US artist Keith Shore). He owns several bars in places as far-flung as Bangkok. Mikkeller is a brand, but one that retains an indefinable Scandinavian cool and an anti-establishment ethos, despite the fact the beer is available in 40 countries all over the world. Plus every year it runs the Copenhagen Beer Celebration, perhaps the most welcoming and enlightening trade festival around.

Mikkeller

Copenhagen, Denmark

CREAM ALE
CREAM ALE

———

20 L / 5 GAL | ABV **5.0%**
OG **1.047** | FG **1.009**

This Cream Ale is one of Mikkeller's less experimental beers, but it's a stunner nonetheless, and still a fairly unconventional example of its type. Cream ale is a relatively rare style originating from the US and is best described as a beautifully balanced cross between a lager and an ale. It's top-fermented like an ale, but with light maltiness and a crisp finish. And it uses flaked corn as an adjunct – it's often negatively associated with macro-brewed US lagers, but here's proof that using it is not always a bad thing. It makes the Cream Ale clean and smooth, providing easy passage for the hops, and the Carapils helps retain a full head. The yeast is a blend of lager and ale varieties with high attenuation and faintly fruity aromas. Some brewers practise cold conditioning with cream ales at the end of fermentation for extra clarity and even more smoothness. Finally, Mikkeller's Cream Ale has a distinctive orangey scent from the liberal use of Amarillo hops: not an 'authentic' trait in this style, but that's what craft brewing is all about. Carbonate it well for a super-refreshing fizz.

- -

GRAIN
Pilsner malt, 1.2kg/2 lbs 10.3oz (30%)

Pale malt, 1.2kg/2 lbs 10.3oz (30%)

Flaked corn, 680g/1 lb 8oz (17%)

Carapils, 260g/9.17oz (6.5%)

Flaked oats, 260g/9.17oz (6.5%)

Vienna malt, 200g/7.05oz (5%)

Munich malt, 200g/7.05oz (5%)

MASH
67C/152F for 75 mins, 74C/165F for 15 mins

HOPS
Columbus 13% AA, 20g/0.7oz, 60 mins

Amarillo 6.5% AA, 25g/0.9oz, 15 mins

Amarillo 6.5% AA, 30g/1.1oz, dry hop

Challenger 7.6% AA, 30g/1.1oz, dry hop

YEAST
White Labs WLP080 Cream Ale Yeast Blend

FERMENT
18-20C/65-68F

Camden Town Brewery

Camden, London, England

INDIA HELLS LAGER
HOPPED HELLES LAGER

---

20 L / 5 GAL | ABV **6.2%**
OG **1.060** | FG **1.012**

Camden Town was founded by Australian Jasper Cuppaidge after he brewed in the cellar of the Horseshoe, a pub in Hampstead, north London. This was 2010, making it a relatively early player in London's craft brewery scene. Since then it's expanded at a huge rate, raising millions of pounds of capital through crowdfunding, and conquering foreign markets. But what sets it apart is its devotion to lager, a style whose reputation suffered horribly at the hands of macro brewers and as such is often overlooked. But done well – and at Camden it always is – a good lager is a beautiful thing. Its Hells is a modern classic, and this India Hells is lager with an even bigger personality – there's a massive hop statement but it's still clear, smooth and balanced. Lagering at home (see p22) needs accurate temperature control, either through an immersion-type cooler or a fridge; master making your own lager though and you'll be a very satisfied brewer and popular come summer. And if you're ever in Camden Town itself, the brewery taproom is great fun to visit.

- -

GRAIN
Weyermann pilsner malt, 4kg/8lbs 13oz (75%)

Munich malt, 1.07kg/2lbs 5.75oz (20%)

Carapils, 270g/9.5oz (5%)

MASH
For single-stage, mash in at 66C/150F for 70 mins. For multi-rest, mash in at 50C/122F, raise to 62C/143F and hold for 60 mins, heat to 72C/161F and hold for 10 minutes. Mash out at 78C/172F

HOPS
Magnum 12.7% AA, 17g/0.6oz, 60 mins (to 25 IBU)

Simcoe 13.9% AA, 9g/0.3oz, 10 mins

Chinook 13.9% AA, 9g/0.3oz, 10 mins

Mosaic 11.2% AA, 11g/0.4oz, 10 mins

Simcoe 13.9% AA, 7g/0.2oz, 0 mins

Chinook 13.9% AA, 17g/0.6oz, 0 mins

Mosaic, 11.2% AA, 9g/0.3oz, 0 mins

Chinook, Simcoe, Mosaic, 80g/2.8oz of each, dry hop

YEAST
Fermentis Saflager W-34/70

FERMENT
10–12C/50–54F until halfway through fermentation, then 14C/57F till the end. When active fermentation is complete leave at 14C/57F for another 72 hours to reduce the diacetyl. After the diacetyl rest is complete, rack on to the dry hops in a separate vessel. Beef up with up to another 2g per litre (0.3oz per gallon) of more of the dry hops if you want to boost the aroma. Continue to hold the beer warm for another 24–48 hours. Then lager it in a beer fridge for approximately 2 weeks

Firestone Walker Brewing Company

Paso Robles, California, USA

UNION JACK
WEST COAST IPA

—

20 L / 5 GAL | ABV **7.5%**
OG **1.068** | FG **1.012**

Adam Firestone comes from a California winemaking background; David Walker is his English brother-in-law. This Sunshine State/rainy Blighty alliance is represented by the bear and the lion on the logo, and by the endlessly award-winning beers (there literally isn't enough space on this page to list the plaudits that have been heaped upon Firestone Walker). The brewery uses a unique and historical Burton upon Trent oak-barrel circulation system for fermenting some of its beers, such as its flagship Double Barrel Ale – the wort spends

six days on wood before moving into steel to finish it off. This peerless and classic West Coast IPA is fermented on steel, however, so you can give it a go at home. It's bullish with bitter hops and garlanded with high-aroma varieties from the US. This is down to the double dry-hopping, a subject brewmaster Matt Brynildson knows pretty much everything about. "I'm a firm believer in short contact time with the hops," he says, "no more than three days. If it starts to taste vegetal, you are on the hops too long. You want clean, juicy-fruit hop oil notes."

GRAIN
2-row American pale malt, 5.18kg/11lbs 6.7oz (86%)

Munich malt, 360g/12.7oz (6%)

Carapils, 300g/10.6oz (5%)

Simpsons crystal malt 30–40L, 180g/6.3oz (3%)

MASH
63C/145F, then 68C/155F to finish conversion

HOPS
Magnum 15% AA, 35g/1.2oz, 90 mins

Cascade 6% AA, 32g/1.1oz, 30 mins

Centennial, 32g/1.1oz, 15 mins

Cascade, 30g/1.1oz, whirlpool

Centennial, 30g/1.1oz, whirlpool

Centennial, Cascade, Simcoe, Amarillo, 75g/2.6oz total ("equal amounts Centennial and Cascade, a bit less of Simcoe and Amarillo"), dry hop 1 at the end of fermentation

As above for dry hop 2, 3 days after first

YEAST
White Labs WLP013 London Ale

FERMENT
19C/66F, then cold crash

Russian River Brewing Company

Santa Rosa, California, USA

RON MEXICO
EXPERIMENTAL-HOPPED AMERICAN PALE ALE

▬

20 L / 5 GAL | ABV 4.5%
OG 1.045 | FG 1.012

There are cult beers, and then there's Pliny the Younger. When this triple IPA is served once a year in February at the Russian River brewpub in Santa Rosa, people travel from far and wide to sample 'the best beer in the world'. But to focus on Pliny is to miss what RRBC is really all about: founder Vinnie Cilurzo is a master of souring and ageing, with 600 barrels at his disposal; he's also one of the most selfless, knowledgeable and respected people brewing today. This recipe is down to his relationship with hop growers and home brewers: he created it for the

2015 Homebrewers Conference in San Diego using HBC-438, an experimental hop so new it doesn't have a name (though it's nicknamed 'Ron Mexico'). Uniquely, 438 will only be available in small quantities for the time being, for keen individuals to get creative with. "A brewer could swap out the HBC-438 for any hop and make a single-hop beer," says Vinnie. "We make a similar beer at RRBC called Hop 2 It and we use it to test new hop varieties." So, hunt down some Ron Mexico, or get some #07270 or 527 or 342, and see why every hop deserves its time in the limelight.

GRAIN
Rahr pale ale malt, 2.01kg/ 4lbs 6.9oz (51.5%)

Rahr 2-row malt, 1.66kg/3lbs 10.6oz (42%)

Weyerman acid malt, 120g/4.2oz (3%)

Breiss Carapils, 100g/3.5oz (2.5%)

Simpsons crystal malt 60L, 30g/1.1oz (1%)

MASH
69C/156F for 60 mins

HOPS
HBC–438 15.7% AA, 3g/0.1oz, 90 mins

HBC–438, 14g/0.5oz, 15 mins

HBC–438, 60g/2.1oz, 0 mins

HBC–438, 73g/2.6oz, dry hop 1 (after 10 days)

HBC–428, 73g/2.6oz, dry hop 2 (pull dry hop 1, after 15 days)

YEAST
WLP001 California Ale

FERMENT
18C/64F; pull yeast after 10 ten days; at 18 days drop to 0C/32F; at 21 days use gelatin or similar to fine, before racking off and carbonating

Brewdog

Ellon, Scotland

—

From a small brewery in Aberdeenshire, northeast Scotland, James Watt and Martin Dickie set out in 2007 with a pretty ambitious aim: to shake the beer world to its core. You'd have to say they succeeded. From the start they've been on a mission against mediocrity in all its beer-related forms, and even if their audacious marketing isn't to your taste, the beers can't fail to be. They're all uncompromisingly flavourful, every one a no-holds-barred celebration of its style, like the hop eruption of Jackhammer IPA or the suave, inky and epic Cocoa Psycho Russian imperial stout. Brewdog has never been afraid to venture to the extremities of craft beer, releasing the better-than-water Nanny State pale ale (0.5% ABV) as well as End of History, a Belgian ale with nettles and juniper which at 55% was stronger than most whiskies and was packaged in taxidermied roadkill. Now there are almost thirty Brewdog bars, from Birmingham to Brazil. Beers exported to more than fifty countries. A brewery in Columbus, Ohio, to send brews in their freshest state all over the States. A record-setting crowdfunding campaign, turning drinkers into investors. One of the fastest-growing brands in the UK. In twenty years' time, the Brewdog story will probably be taught in MBA courses, but more importantly, Brewdog beer will probably still be awesome.

Brewdog

Ellon, Scotland

PUNK IPA
IPA

—

20 L / 5 GAL | ABV **5.60%**
OG **1.054** | FG **1.012**

If you're not drinking a Punk IPA right now, you probably know someone who is. It's sold in shops, supermarkets, off-licences, bottle shops, bars and pubs the world over. This is the beer that started it all for Brewdog back in 2007: not many people in buttoned-up Britain had ever tasted a beer so fresh, so confident, so rammed full of flavour with every sip. Buttoned-up Britain was a bit scared, to be honest, although Punk didn't take long to win them over, and it won over loads of other countries to boot. It's a true craft beer classic: refreshing but involving; strong enough to make itself known but friendly enough to enjoy a few of; gushing with pine, tropical fruit, flowers and citrus, all that's great about hops – a result of the generous handfuls of six strains including the Pacific Northwestern Ahtanum and Cascade, and the peerless Kiwi Nelson Sauvin. The malt backbone is steady but simple enough to give them all a chance to shine. If you can make your own version even 10% as good as the original, you'll be a hero. In a world where bland beer fills most glasses, Punk IPA is still a rebel.

- -

GRAIN
Pale ale malt, 4.4kg/9lbs 11.2oz (92.5%)

Caramalt, 360g/12.7oz (7.5%)

MASH
Mash in at 65C/149F, rest for 15 mins. Raise to 72C/162F, rest for 15 mins (iodine test, see p37). Mash off at 78C/172F

HOPS
Ahtanum, 2g/0.07oz, 80 mins

Chinook, 8g/0.3oz, 15 mins

Ahtanum, 10g/0.35oz, 15 mins

Ahtanum, 6g/0.21oz, whirlpool

Chinook, 4g/0.14oz, whirlpool

Simcoe, 10g/0.35oz, whirlpool

Nelson Sauvin, 5g/0.15oz, whirlpool

Ahtanum, 40g/1.4oz, dry hop

Chinook, 50g/1.8oz, dry hop

Simcoe, 40g/1.4oz, dry hop

Nelson Sauvin, 20g/0.7oz, dry hop

Cascade, 40g/1.4oz, dry hop

YEAST
Wyeast 1056 American Ale

FERMENT
19C/66F for 5 days, dry hop at 14C/57F for 5 days, mature at 0C/32F for 15 days

Siren Craft Brew

Finchampstead, Berkshire, England

UNDERCURRENT
OATMEAL PALE ALE

---

20 L / 5 GAL | ABV **4.5%**
OG **1.044** | FG **1.010**

Within two years of Darron Anley's inaugural mash-in, his Berkshire brewery had been named second-best new brewery in the world in Ratebeer.com's annual drinkers' survey. The love Siren receives is largely down to its commitment to courageously un-traditional beer, open-mindedness and a total disregard for brewing boundaries. Limited-edition releases have included a peach cream IPA brewed with Omnipollo (see p130) and a barrel-aged hopfenweizen with Brettanomyces yeast. Experimentation has to be built on a solid understanding of what works in a brewhouse – and this Undercurrent is a prime example of an overperforming everyday beer. As well as wheat malt and Carahell to add body and colour, it uses oat malt, a not-often-seen grain with a really warm flavour – it works well in all sorts of beers, but in this pale ale it's a revelation. This is also the only recipe in the book that uses the Pacific Northwestern Palisade hop, which brings 'sweet nectar' fruit along with herbs and freshly mown meadow flavours.

GRAIN
Maris Otter pale malt, 2.66kg/5lbs 13.8oz (71%)

Malted oats, 520g/1lb 2.3oz (14%)

Wheat malt, 260g/9.2oz (7%)

Carahell, 260g/9.2oz (7%)

Caraaroma, 40g/1.4oz (1%)

MASH
68C/145F for 60 mins (Siren recommends recirculating for last 45 minutes, if you can)

HOPS
(70 minute boil)

Magnum, 7g/0.3oz, 60 mins

Cascade, 20g/0.7oz, 10 mins

Cascade, 20g/0.7oz, 0 mins

Palisade, 16g/0.6oz, 0 mins

Columbus, 12g/0.4oz, 0 mins

YEAST
Fermentis US–05 American Ale

FERMENT
20C/68F

Oskar Blues Brewery

Lyons, Colorado, USA

DALE'S PALE ALE
AMERICAN PALE ALE

---

20 L / 5 GAL | ABV **6.5%**
OG **1.066** | FG **1.015**

If you're a brewer called Dale then you pretty much have to make a pale ale and then call it Dale's Pale Ale. Oskar Blues founder Dale Katechis did just that with his citrussy hop-loaded signature brew, then he went one step further – he put it in a can. That was in 2002, when canned beer meant gassy, ricey, mainstream and bland. Now, beer crafters the world over are saying "yes we can" and packaging their brews in protective aluminium. Dale's was the first craft beer in a can, a true pioneer, but that's not the only thing that makes it great. The copious amounts of classic US craft beer 'C' hops (Cascade, Centennial, Columbus) brings a recognisably grapefruit/flowery/herbal flavour, but without the dry-hopping present in more aggressive American IPAs; the relatively complex malt bill provides a sweet body that sits side-by-side with them in perfect harmony. It's everything an American pale ale should be: balanced and crisp, charismatic and friendly, there for you any time of day. DPA is the perfect toast to a real revolution in beermaking.

GRAIN
North American 2-row pale malt 2L, 4.68kg/10lbs 5.1oz (80%)

Crystal malt 25L, 590g/ 1lb 4.8oz (10%)

Munich malt 10L, 470g/ 1lb 0.6oz (8%)

Crystal malt 85L, 120g/ 4.2oz (2%)

MASH
69C/156F for 60 mins

HOPS
(90 minute boil)

Columbus 14% AA, 14g/0.5oz, 80 mins, to 25 IBU

Cascade, 14g/0.5oz, 25 mins

Columbus, 17g/0.6oz, 10 mins

Centennial, 45g/1.6oz, whirlpool

YEAST
Wyeast WLP001 California Ale

FERMENT
Primary at 18C/64F, then cold condition for around 10 days

SPECIAL INSTRUCTIONS
Dale's is brewed with soft water with a target wort Chloride:Sulfate ratio of 1:1

The Celt Experience

Caerphilly, Wales

SILURES
MUNICH PALE ALE WITH SPRUCE

—

20 L / 5 GAL | ABV **4.6%**
OG **1.044** | FG **1.008**

Celt Experience is not a normal brewery. Founder Tom Newman takes inspiration from the mythology of the Welsh Celts and has a deep connection to the land. His beers include the brilliant Tail-less Black Sow, a herb-infused pale ale named after a ghostly pig of folk legend. Wild yeasts are harvested from sites of spiritual significance; mugwort and yarrow foraged from forests. Silures (after an ancient tribe from southeast Wales) uses what Tom calls his hop druid: "It eats hops for dinner," he says. You probably don't have a hop druid. But you could buy a percolator, or make one – it's a vessel with a sealed lid which allows wort to flow through and it extracts huge amounts of aroma from steeped hops within (similar to a hopback: see p24). 'Generous' amounts are called for – about as much as you can fit in. A note on spruce tips: pick them locally if possible. You can buy them online, and if you don't live near a native forest it may be your best option. It won't have the same magic, but you'll still appreciate their uniquely resinous, floral character.

GRAIN
Pale ale malt, 3.6kg/7lbs 15oz (92%)

Munich malt, 160g/5.6oz (4%)

Wheat malt, 160g/5.6oz (4%)

MASH
64.5C/148F for 60 mins

HOPS
(60 minute boil)

Magnum or similar bittering hop, 25g/0.88oz, 40 mins, to hit 36 IBU

Centennial, 67g/2.4oz, 5 mins

Citra, 17g/0.6oz, 5 mins

Simcoe, 34g/1.2oz, 0 mins

Citra, Centennial and Simcoe in the hop druid (see above!)

Simcoe, 34g/1.2oz, dry hop

YEAST
Fermentis US-05 American Ale

FERMENT
20C/68F

OTHER INGREDIENTS
Foraged spruce tips, 17g/0.7oz, at flameout, steeped for 5 mins

Trouble Brewing

Kildare, Ireland

HIDDEN AGENDA
PALE ALE

---

20 L / 5 GAL | ABV **4.5%**
OG **1.043** | FG **1.009**

There's a joke about drinking in Irish pubs. You've got two choices: a pint of Guinness, or a half-pint of Guinness. It's true that the black stuff flows like water in Ireland, and thanks to its ubiquity Irish beer has a bit of a one-dimensional reputation worldwide. But a growing band of brewers all over the country are looking beyond stout to give beer lovers something to get excited about. Trouble, based in County Kildare (and just down the road from Arthur Guinness's birthplace), is doing just that by making classy beers ranging from a relaxed golden ale to a cherry chocolate stout. Hidden Agenda isn't especially Irish in outlook but is a deadly drop all the same. It's a relaxed and supremely drinkable sunny-day pale ale, with a fairly simple objective: crisp and complex malts provide a launchpad for a faceful of fruit-salad Aussie hops. The relatively new Vic Secret strain and its compatriot Summer are all about apricots, peaches, melons and citrus; melanoidin is a speciality grain which in small quantities adds a subtle red colour and a malty taste. Who needs Guinness?

GRAIN
Pale ale malt, 2.75kg/6lbs 1oz (72%)

Munich malt, 760g/1lb 10.8oz (20%)

Melanoidin, 150g/5.3oz (4%)

Carapils, 80g/2.8oz (2%)

Crystal malt 57L, 80g/2.8oz (2%)

MASH
66C/150F for 60 mins

HOPS
Magnum 12.7% AA, 9g/0/3oz, 60 mins

Summer 5.3% AA, 26g/0.9oz, 10 mins

Summer 5.3% AA, 26g/0.9oz, 5 mins

Vic Secret 15.8% AA, 39g/ 1.4oz, 0 mins

Vic Secret 15.8% AA, 39g/1.4oz, dry hop

YEAST
Fermentis US-05 American Ale

FERMENT
20C/68F

Omnipollo

Stockholm, Sweden

———

With a team made up of a talented graphic designer (Karl Grandin) and a talented brewer (Henok Fentie), it was pretty much inevitable that Omnipollo would produce beer that looked as good as it tastes. See the labels below for proof of the first bit, see your local bottle shop for proof of the second. What wasn't inevitable, but is the result of tireless creativity and hard work, is that their beers are some of the most sought-after in the world. Omnipollo, like so many in Scandinavia, is a gypsy brewery: many are made at the high-tech De Proefbrouwerij in Belgium, others are born of collaborations (with Siren, Evil Twin and Stillwater, among others); the imagination, though, is all theirs. Nathalius is an 8% imperial IPA brewed with rice and corn, ingredients usually shunned by craft brewers: all the more reason to use them. Yellow Belly, brewed with Buxton Brewery, is a 'peanut butter biscuit stout' without peanut butter or biscuits, one of the most sought-after beers in the world. Mazarin, the one with the covetable candle bottle, is simply a pale ale, but maybe the best one you'll ever try.

Omnipollo

Stockholm, Sweden

4:21
DOUBLE RASPBERRY/VANILLA SMOOTHIE IPA

—

20 L / **5** GAL | ABV **6%**
OG **1.054** | FG **1.010**

Along with the likes of Mikkeller and To Øl, Omnipollo represents everything that's exciting, nonconformist and forward-thinking about Scandinavian brewing. It's run by homebrewer-turned-pro Henok Fentie and graphic designer Karl Grandin, who's responsible for perhaps the coolest beer art in the world – the bottles are so smart you'll want to hang on to them long after the last sip. There's no actual Omnipollo brewery, but instead the pair's creations are made all around the world, with plenty of collaborations along the way. This 4:21 is part of Omnipollo's Magic

Numbers series, a set of small-batch, limited-edition beers which blast off even further into the unexplored reaches of brewing. It's super-fruity and sharp from the raspberries and wheat, but the vanilla and lactose gives it a creamy, almost thick character – hence the 'smoothie' in the name. Lactose is almost completely unfermentable with beer yeast, so won't increase the ABV; it does increase the gravity of the wort though. And the late, heavy hop additions add a ton of flavour and even a fair amount of IBUs. A genuinely groundbreaking beer!

- -

GRAIN
Pilsner malt, 2.65kg/5lbs 13.5oz (60%)

Wheat, 880g/1lb 15oz (20%)

Flaked oats, 440g/15.5oz (10%)

MASH
67C/152F for 75 mins

HOPS
(60 minute boil)

Mosaic, 27g/1oz, 10 mins

Mosaic, 67g/2.4oz, whirlpool

Mosaic, 200g/7oz, dry hop for 3 days

YEAST
Fermentis S-04 English Ale

FERMENT
19C/66F

OTHER INGREDIENTS
Dextrose, 440g/15.5oz (10%), in the boil

Lactose, after the boil, to raise the OG by 3P (about 12–13 specific gravity points); around 700g/ 1lb 8oz

Fresh raspberries, 1.3kg/2lbs 13.9oz, and 2.5 vanilla pods sliced down the middle, after primary fermentation, before dry hopping

Yeastie Boys

Wellington, New Zealand

DIGITAL IPA
NZ-HOPPED IPA

▬▬

20 L / 5 GAL | ABV **5.7%**
OG **1.056** | FG **1.013**

There might be a better-named brewery in the world than Yeastie Boys, but it's hard to imagine. It started as a part-time project for Stu McKinley and Sam Possenniskie in Wellington, but such was the quality of their beers that they were soon the toast of the NZ brewing scene. Their Pot Kettle Black (the most-awarded Kiwi beer) doesn't just blur the lines between black IPAs and hoppy porters, it pretty much proves there needn't be any lines there in the first place. The Yeasties' lean business model sees them planning their beers from a Wellington base while the brewing is done elsewhere. Stu relocated half a world away to London in 2015 to kick off the brand's operations in the Northern Hemisphere – resulting in fresher beer which is somehow still Kiwi through-and-through, despite being made over 10,000 miles away (look for the Gunnamatta earl-grey-infused IPA). Their story is a paradigm of modern craft brewing, and this Digital IPA is a paragon of modern IPAs: a balance between caramel malts and lots and lots of lovely NZ hops.

- -

GRAIN
Pilsner malt, 2.48kg/5lbs 7.5oz (52%)

Vienna malt, 2.06kg/4lbs 8.7oz (43.5%)

Gladiator malt (or Carapils), 210g/7.1oz (4.5%)

MASH
66C/151F for 60 mins

HOPS
Pacific Jade pellets 13.4% AA, 35g/1.2oz, 60 mins

Motueka pellets 7.3% AA, 8g/0.3oz, 10 mins

Nelson Sauvin pellets 12.1% AA, 8g/0.3oz, 10 mins

Southern Cross pellets 13.6% AA, 8g/0.3oz, 0 mins

Motueka pellets 7.3% AA, 40g/1.4oz, 0 mins

Nelson Sauvin pellets 12.1% AA, 8g/0.3oz, 0 mins

Southern Cross pellets 13.6% AA, 17g/0.6oz, dry hop 1

Nelson Sauvin pellets 12.1% AA, 8g/0.3oz, dry hop 1

Motueka pellets 7.3% AA, 17g/0.6oz, dry hop 1

Southern Cross pellets 13.6% AA, 8g/0.3oz, dry hop 2, 4 days after first

Nelson Sauvin pellets 12.1% AA, 4g/0.14oz, dry hop 2

Motueka pellets 7.3% AA, 17g/0.6oz, dry hop 2

YEAST
Fermentis US–05 American Ale

FERMENT
18C/65F

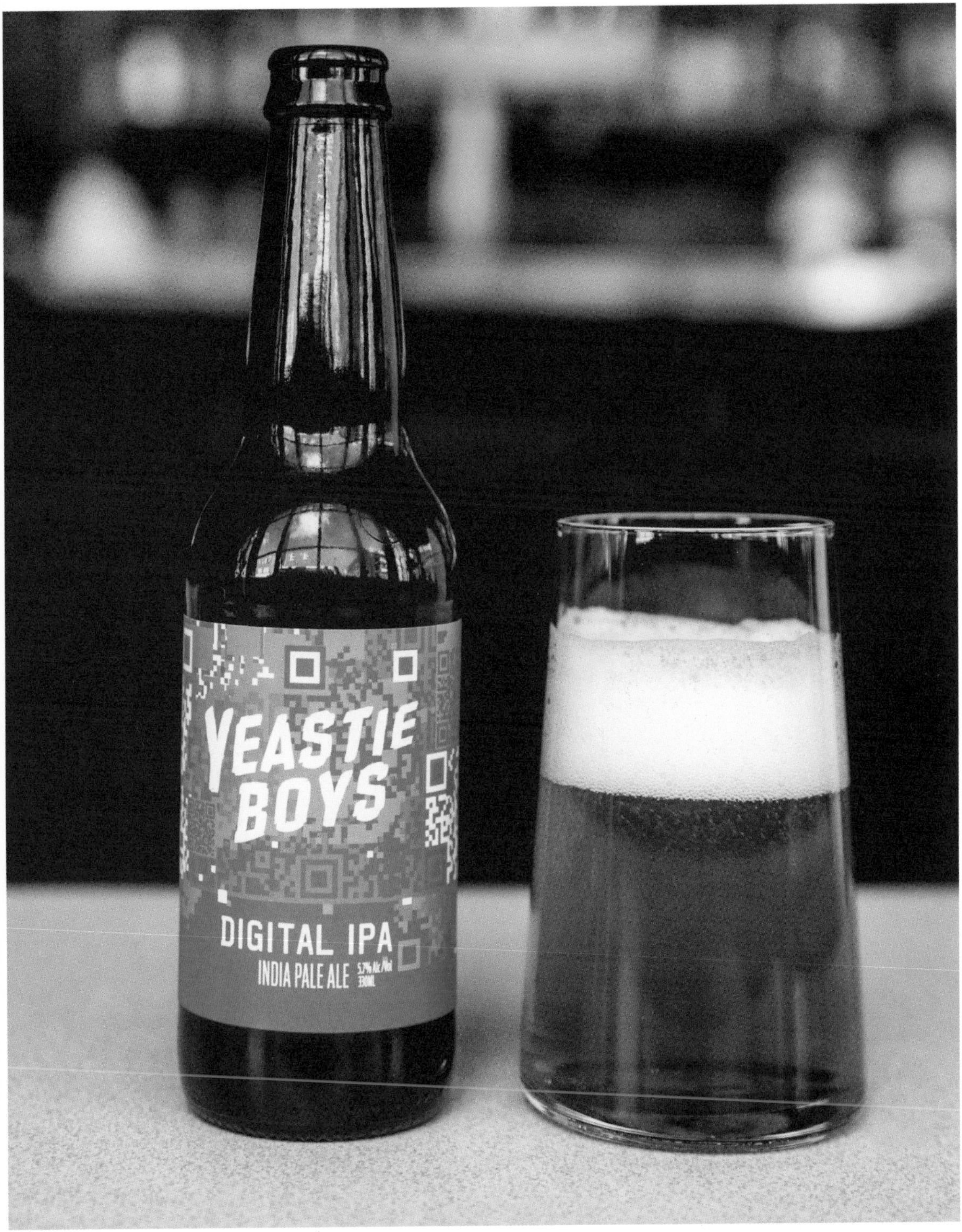
YEASTIE BOYS
DIGITAL IPA
INDIA PALE ALE
5.7% Alc/Vol
330ML

Young Henrys

Newtown, New South Wales, Australia

NATURAL LAGER
KELLERBIER

━━━

20 L / 5 GAL | ABV **4.2%**
OG **1.042** | FG **1.010**

A kellerbier is an ancient German style, fairly rare outside the country, which can be top- or bottom-fermented, but is also unfiltered and boldly loaded with aromatic hops. NSW brewery Young Henrys stays true to the tradition, including Munich malt to give this Natural Lager an authentic amber tint. Instead of Hallertauer or Mittelfrüh, however, they've used Summer, Helga and Sylva – all relatives of classic European strains that emigrated Down Under and grew extra fruity under the Aussie sun. The result is unpretentious, gently citrussy and perfectly refreshing, hazy too from the wheat and lack of filtering. It also uses Cry Havoc yeast, which works at lager and ale temperatures. Young Henrys was founded by two friends in 2012 – it *is* still young, but something of a prodigy: a consistently exacting core range (which also includes Real Ale English best bitter) is brewed alongside out-there creations like a witbier made with mussels (really), and I Should Coco, a chocolate truffle stout. There are now YH breweries in two more Australian states, so the beer's as fresh in Sydney as it is in Perth.

- -

GRAIN
Pilsner malt, 3.2kg/7lbs 0.9oz (86%)

Pale wheat malt, 250g/ 8.8oz (7%)

Munich malt, 250g/ 8.8oz (7%)

MASH
67C/152F for 50 mins

HOPS
(60 minute boil)

Summer, 15g/0.5oz, first wort hops

Summer, 20g/0.7oz, 5 mins

Sylva, 20g/0.7oz, whirlpool

Helga, 20g/0/7oz, whirlpool

YEAST
White Labs WLP862 Cry Havoc

FERMENT
16C/61F until gravity reaches 1.020, then let temperature rise naturally to 22C/71F. Wait 2 days after final gravity is reached then chill for 7 days before priming and packaging

Stout, porter & black

—

The difference between stout, porter and black IPA is a source of debate, and craft brewers love blurring the lines. Save yourself the arguments, and just make and drink them. Heavily roasted malts give a midnight-black colour and chocolate, coffee, and dark fruit notes, which stand up well to high alcohol, big hops and complementary added flavours.

Dark Star Brewing Company

West Sussex, England

ESPRESSO
DARK COFFEE BEER

——

20 L / 5 GAL | ABV **4.2%**
OG **1.048** | FG **1.014**

Reasons to love Sussex brewery Dark Star:
1) It sponsors the British National Homebrew Competition and every year brews the winning beer for commercial release. 2) It contributes to all sorts of pub and beer-related charities through the Dark Star Foundation. 3) Since 1994 it has brilliantly combined the best of British brewing traditions (plenty of cask ale) with New World ingredients and attitudes. 4) All its beer is just great, including this Espresso black beer. It's maybe not quite hefty enough to be called a stout, as the only really dark grain involved here is the roasted barley. It's a very useful and distinctive grain to use in heavier beers, and is highly baked in a drum, giving it almost coffee-like characteristics. Roasted barley adds a beautifully sweet aspect to cushion the bitter jolt from the ground coffee. Other coffee-based beers may use more ground beans by weight, but in Dark Star's version it's more of a background brew within a brew. In other words, maybe not a substitute for your morning cup of joe, but a fine beer with layers of subtle blackness.

GRAIN
Pale ale malt, 3kg/6lbs 10oz (70%)

Wheat, 690g/1lb 8oz (16%)

Roasted barley, 470g/1lb 1oz (11%)

Caramalt, 130g/4.6oz (3%)

MASH
67C/153F for 60 mins

HOPS
Challenger, 30g/1.1oz, 60 mins

Challenger, 11g/0.4oz, 0 mins

YEAST
Danstar Nottingham Ale or White Labs WLP039 Nottingham Ale

FERMENT
20C/68F

OTHER INGREDIENTS
Freshly ground Arabica coffee, the best you can get your hands on, 22g/0.8oz at the end of the boil. Leave as you would aroma hops before transferring to fermenter. Best to use a fine bag – coffee grounds are messy to clean up!

Beavertown Brewery

Tottenham, London, England

In the few short years since Beavertown Brewery was founded by Logan Plant in a London bar, it's come a long way. Out of the basement of Duke's Brew & Que, his barbecue restaurant, into dedicated premises in nearby Hackney Wick; then outgrowing them and moving into an even bigger space in Tottenham. And instead of just making beer for the pulled-pork-munching diners in Duke's, Beavertown exports to twenty countries around the world from its north London base. One thing has remained the same and fuelled its expansion – a range of amazing beers unfettered by convention and founded on fearless experimentation. A few were brewed in the pub cellar and went on to form the core range (the spicy 8-Ball Rye IPA, say, or Smog Rocket); others are collaborations with some of the world's most innovative brewers or limited-release one-offs (a bramley apple saison, for example). Some redefine 'cult' beer: the annual arrival of Beavertown's 7.2% blood orange IPA is heralded by a stampede towards the bars and bottle shops lucky enough to have some in stock. There's also a canning line for the core beers: a commitment to freshness and lower environmental impact. And central to the Beavertown success is the identity, which has been clear since the start. Nick Dwyer worked in Duke's and presented Logan with a few sketches inspired by his brews: "If you ever need labels for them, here are some ideas." Now Nick is the brewery's creative director and his much-lauded designs are seen on cans by eager Beaver lovers in markets as diverse as Australia, the US and Hong Kong.

Beavertown Brewery

Tottenham, London, England

SMOG ROCKET
SMOKED PORTER

▬▬▬

20 L / 5 GAL | ABV **5.4%**
OG **1.057** | FG **1.014**

This is one of Beavertown founder Logan Plant's original homebrew recipes, and it has survived the journey from kitchen kit to 50 hectolitres pretty much intact. Smog Rocket's hugely diverse grain bill – nine varieties! – creates a complex and involving porter, with an enveloping darkness that allows the smoke to curl in and out among the roasted coffee, burnt toffee, smouldering peat and dark chocolate flavours. Too much smokiness in any brew recipe could lead to an overpowering ashtray sensation rather than a gently welcoming wisp of campfire, but the proportion of smoked malt here is carefully balanced by its mash mates. The combination of crystal, brown, chocolate, cara and black, even in low quantities, all bring something unique to the mix. Hops in this beer are there mainly for equilibrium (the IBUs are fairly low), although the delicately smoky notes sometimes picked up in Chinook make themselves known too. Beavertown cans almost its whole range and they're available around the world now, so if you see a Smog Rocket, snap it up.

GRAIN
Pale malt, 1.53kg/3lbs 5.6oz (30%)

Beechwood-smoked malt, 1.53kg/3lbs 5.6oz (30%)

Munich malt, 560g/1lb 3.75oz (11%)

Flaked oats, 410g/14.5oz (8%)

Dark crystal malt, 310g/10.9oz (6%)

Brown malt, 310g/10.9oz (6%)

Chocolate malt, 310g/10.9oz (6%)

Caramalt, 100g/3.5oz (2%)

Black malt, 50g/1.8oz (1%)

MASH
66C/150F for 60 mins

HOPS
Magnum, 8g/0.3oz, 60 mins

Chinook, 14g/0.5oz, 30 mins

YEAST
Fermentis US-05 American Ale

FERMENT
19C/66F

Brouwerij de Molen

Bodegraven, Netherlands

SPANNING & SENSATIE
SPICED IMPERIAL STOUT

▬

20 L / 5 GAL | ABV **9.8%**
OG **1.102** | FG **1.028**

The brewing of the Netherlands might be historically overshadowed by its neighbours Belgium and Germany, but under these conditions a microbrewing industry thrives, free from any need to even pretend to compete with the likes of Heineken. De Molen ('the Windmill') is the most consistently eclectic, bold and brilliant, notable not just in Holland but across the world for an enormous roster of rarely repeated beers with inspiration from classic European and US styles. Spanning & Sensatie ('Thrills & Spills') is described as 'Imperial Stout-ish', and it's certainly strong, panther-black and loaded with roasted malts; such turbo-charged porters are never short of flavour, but this is enhanced daringly with cacao nibs, chilli and salt. The result is something like a molten Aztec dark chocolate bar, with liquorice and coffee undertones, a warming current of alcohol and spice and an intriguing tang at the end. However, the additions are nothing without a good beer, and imperial stout isn't easy to brew, so take your time: vorlauf slowly, sparge slowly, run off slowly, pitch yeast heavily, then age… slowly.

- -

GRAIN
Belgian pilsner malt, 4.03kg/ 8lbs 14oz (43%)

Smoked malt, 1.22kg/2lbs 11oz (13%)

Brown malt, 940g/2lbs 1oz (10%)

Crystal malt 60L, 940g/2lb 1oz (10%)

Flaked oats, 840g/1lb 13.6oz (9%)

Acid malt, 750g/1lb 10.5oz (8%)

Chocolate malt, 520g/1lb 2.3oz (5.5%)

Roasted barley, 140g/4.9oz (1.5%)

MASH
69C/156F for 60 mins

HOPS
Columbus, 60g/2.1oz, 90 mins

Saaz, 8g/0.3oz, 10 mins

YEAST
Fermentis US-05 American Ale, 2 packs

OTHER INGREDIENTS
Cacao nibs, crushed lightly, 100g/3.5oz

½ Madame Jeanette chilli pepper

Sea salt, 10g/0.35oz

Put all in a sanitised bag and add after primary fermentation for up to a week

Odell Brewing Company

Fort Collins, Colorado, USA

CUTTHROAT PORTER
PORTER

▬▬▬

20 L / 5 GAL | ABV 5.1%
OG 1.050 | FG 1.015

Doug Odell was making beer at home back when most of today's craft brewers were drinking nothing stronger than milk. Now he's one of the most respected brewers in the country, and his canny expansion from Colorado across the world is based on a foundation of great beer with a perfect balance between experimentation and consistency. His take on a 90/- Scottish ale has been an Odell constant since 1989 and is a modern classic; so too this creamy Cutthroat Porter, named after an endangered Coloradan trout. Technically speaking, it's more of a 'brown' than a robust porter, having a lower percentage of the highest-roast malts than some other examples. The mash temperature is high to create a full body in the beer, and the English ale yeast is low in esters and clean, but leaves a mild sweetness that suits the style. It's deep and dark, with plenty of coffee, chocolate, tobacco and burnt flavours; this, along with its English East Kent Goldings and Fuggles at flameout (hops are meant to be subtle in this style) plus easygoing ABV, makes it an accessible and sessionable porter.

- -

GRAIN
Pale ale malt, 3.78kg/8lbs 5.3oz (79%)

Caramalt, 270g/9.5oz (5.5%)

Chocolate malt, 220g/7.8oz (4.5%)

Crystal malt 53–60L,170g/6oz (3.5%)

Amber malt, 170g/6oz (3.5%)

Munich malt, 110g/3.9oz (2.5%)

Roasted barley, 60g/1.8oz (1.5%)

MASH
68C/154F for 60 mins

HOPS
Nugget, Cascade or any good bittering hop, 24g/0.85oz, 60 mins, to hit 40 IBUs

East Kent Goldings, 12g/0/4oz, 0 minutes

Fuggles, 10g/0.35oz, 0 minutes

YEAST
A clean, low-ester yeast, such as WLP002 English Ale

FERMENT
20C/68F

Deschutes Brewery

Bend, Oregon, USA

BLACK BUTTE PORTER
PORTER

20 L / 5 GAL | ABV **5.2%**
OG **1.057** | FG **1.019**

Deschutes is a beacon of righteous Oregon brewing. Named after the local river, it's been based in Bend since 1988, when it opened as a humble brewpub. Bend is a town surrounded by place names familiar to brewers the world over thanks to the state's famous hops, including the Cascade Mountains and Willamette National Forest; Deschutes is now one of the biggest craft breweries in USA. Forming a solid base to a series of experimentals and seasonals (including the much-anticipated fresh-hopped IPA in winter) is a core range that includes this Black Butte Porter, a tribute to an extinct volcano in Deschutes National Forest. For a long-established Pacific Northwestern brewery to have a porter as its flagship brew is brave, but this rich, sweet and creamy beer is every bit as drinkable as a pale ale. Bravo is a fairly new (2006) hop from local breeding fields which brings high alpha acid levels and a lightly fruity aroma; it's augmented with the most-used craft hop variety in the US (Cascade) plus Tettnang. A weeknight porter with enough character to see you through to Saturday.

GRAIN
2-row pale malt, 2.8kg/ 6lbs 2.8oz (63%)

Chocolate malt, 450g/1lb (10%)

Wheat malt, 400g/14oz (9%)

Crystal malt C75, 400g/14oz (9%)

Carapils, 400g/14oz (9%)

MASH
Mash in at 54C/130F and hold for 10 mins. Raise temperature to 69C/157F and rest for 30 mins. Mash off at 75C/168F and hold for at least 5 mins

HOPS
Bravo 14% AA, 14g/0.5oz, 60 mins

Cascade 6% AA, 14g/0.5oz, 30 mins

Tettnang 5% AA, 28g/1oz, 5 mins

YEAST
White Labs WLP002 English Ale or Wyeast 1187 Ringwood Ale

FERMENT
17C/63F

Ninkasi Brewing Company

Eugene, Oregon, USA

OATIS
OATMEAL STOUT

▬

20 L / 5 GAL | ABV **7%**
OG **1.072** | FG **1.020**

Oregon is a pretty good place to be a craft beer fan, as you can tell from the dozens of breweries dedicated to keeping the Beaver State flush with good things to drink. And although Portland may have more breweries per head, Eugene is a pretty good city to be a craft beer fan too. As well as Ninkasi, beermakers here include Hop Valley, whose cans burst with the flavours of the region's precious hop crop, as well as Oakshire and a whole load more. Ninkasi is a refreshing alternative to the skulls-and-heavy-metal-asskicking that typifies a lot of brewing: it's named after the Sumerian goddess of beer, its 'Beer is Love' programme supports charity in a big way, its spent grain goes to feed some (lucky) naturally reared cows. And it makes fine beer: Oatis is a tribute to the brewery's mascot dog Otis, and while he might not be able to enjoy it, the rest of us can appreciate the silky smooth mouthfeel, the deep dark roastiness and the balance of sweet malt and mildly bitter Nugget hops. Ninkasi also makes a Vanilla Oatis, which has an extra creamy depth.

- -

GRAIN
2-row pale malt, 4.86kg/10lbs 11.4oz (74%)

Chocolate malt, 390g/13.8oz (6%)

Crystal malt, 390g/13.8oz (6%)

Flaked oats, 390g/13.8oz (6%)

Vienna malt, 330g/11.6oz (5%)

Roasted barley, 130g/4.6oz (2%)

Rice hulls, 70g/2.5oz (1%)

MASH
67C/152F for 40 mins

HOPS
Nugget, 23g/0.8oz, 60 mins

Nugget, 23g/0.8 oz, 30 mins

YEAST
White Labs WLP005 British Ale

FERMENT
20C/68F for 3-7 days; hold for 2 days at final gravity; chill to 0C/32F for 7-10 days

Põhjala

Tallin, Estonia

ODENSHOLM
IMPERIAL PORTER

▬▬

20 L / 5 GAL | ABV 9%
OG **1.083** | FG **1.019**

For most people outside the country, Estonian beer means Viru, a pilsner whose unusual tower-shaped bottle somewhat overshadows its contents in terms of interest. Not now: there's a real craft scene, with young breweries across the Eastern European state producing memorable beers. Põhjala is based in the capital Tallinn and headed up by Christopher Pilkington, a Scottish brewer once of Brewdog (see p118). Põhjala teamed up with another northern powerhouse, Norway's Lervig (see p93), to create this midwinter-black imperial porter. Such supercharged stouts are often described in terms of 'size', and this one's so big it has dark corners to get lost in. The rye and chocolate rye give it a spicy kick, while the long maturation at low temperature take the warming alcohol and bitter hops into deep new dimensions. Make sure your yeast is healthy – it will have a lot of work to do. Christopher gives his beer a further rest in a pinot noir barrel, which if you can do you should: "It makes the dark berry flavours of the carafa malt and chocolate rye merge perfectly." One to get you through a cold night.

- -

GRAIN
Viking pale malt, 4.84kg/ 10lb 10.7oz (62.5%)

Rye malt, 1.55kg/3lb 6.7oz (20%)

Carafa Special Type-II malt, 500g/1lb 1.6oz (6.5%)

Chocolate rye malt, 390g/13.8oz (5%)

Special B malt, 390g/13.8oz (5%)

MASH
68C/154F for 45 mins

HOPS
Magnum or CTZ, 50g/1.76oz, 60 mins

Chinook, 20g/0.7oz, 0 mins

YEAST
White Labs WLP090 San Diego Super

FERMENT
19C/66F, then 4 weeks maturation at 0C/32F

OTHER INGREDIENTS
Demerara sugar, 80g/2.8oz (1%), halfway through boil

The Kernel Brewery

Bermondsey, London, England

EXPORT INDIA PORTER
EXPORT INDIA PORTER

▬

20 L / 5 GAL | ABV **6%**
OG **1.060** | FG **1.016**

This is not subjective, it's true: the Kernel makes incredible beer. Everything about it speaks of simplicity: brown hand-printed labels with minimal information (no tasting notes or boasts of how the contents will change your life); a concise range of beers, ever changing but always true to their style and perfectly crafted. They're mainly heartily hopped IPAs and pale ales, plus the easy-drinking Table Beer, sours and reinventions of historical London styles like mighty stouts and porters. This Export India Porter is free with the hops, just as they would have been in the nineteenth century. And the varieties aren't specified. That's not secrecy, it's because there are no fixed recipes. "We like to experiment with different hop varieties," says founder Evin O'Riordain. "They can create very different flavours when combined with darker malts, which is fascinating. Bramling Cross is our favourite for a more traditional British character. Columbus works very well for a brasher, New World character." Use the recipe here as an inspiration, aim for about 48 IBU. The Kernel uses hard London water, with extra calcium chloride.

- -

GRAIN
Maris Otter malt, 3.96kg/ 8lbs 11.7oz (75.5%)

Brown malt, 370g/13oz (7%)

Chocolate malt, 370g/13oz (7%)

Dark crystal malt, 370g/13oz (7%)

Black malt, 180g/6.3oz (3.5%)

MASH
Around 69C/156F for 60 mins

HOPS
12% AA, 10g/0.35oz, first wort hop

12% AA, 10g/0.35oz, 15 mins

12% AA, 14g/0.5oz, 10 minutes

12% AA, 20g/0.7oz, 5 minutes

12% AA, 40g/1.4oz, dry hop for 3 days before bottling/kegging

YEAST
Kernel uses a house yeast, but you could use something locally appropriate like White Labs WLP013 London Ale

FERMENT
20C/68F, then condition for 10–14 days at 15–20C/59–68F for the beer to carbonate properly

To Øl

Copenhagen, Denmark

BLACK BALL
PORTER

———

20 L / 5 GAL | ABV **7.1%**
OG **1.084** | FG **1.024**

Non-Danish speakers – it's pronounced 'too eul' and translates into one of the best phrases in any language: 'two beers'. In 2005, founders Tobias and Tore, then at school, had a cool science teacher who just happened to be future Mikkeller supremo Mikkel Borg Bjergsø (see p108). United by a disillusion with mainstream Danish beer (you surely know which one), the trio began brewing in the school kitchen after hours. The school was presumably totally fine with this arrangement, and it's worked out pretty well for beer lovers too. If you were ever in any doubt that Denmark is probably the best place to live in the world, that story has doubtless convinced you. In the progressive way, To Øl has no premises – it's a gypsy brewery – but still manages to make an increasingly adventurous range of beautifully designed beers. And this Black Ball is no ordinary porter: the multifarious malt bill is nuanced and involving, the unrefined sugar adds further intrigue, and the plentiful hops illuminate the dark depths. Hoppy porter, black IPA or India stout? When it tastes this good, who cares.

- -

GRAIN
Pilsner malt, 4.15kg/9lbs 2.4oz (57%)

Roasted barley, 700g/1lb 8.7oz (9.5%)

Smoked malt, 610g/1lb 5.5oz (8%)

Flaked oats, 530g/1lb 2.7oz (7%)

Chocolate malt, 440g/15.5oz (6%)

Caramunich, 350g/12.4oz (5%)

Brown malt, 210g/7.4oz (3%)

MASH
67C/152F for 60 mins, 72C/ 161F for 15 mins

HOPS
Simcoe 13% AA, 26g/0.9oz, 60 mins

Simcoe 13% AA, 20g/0.7oz, 15 mins

Centennial 10% AA, 20g/0.7oz, 10 mins

Cascade 6.5%AA, 30g/1oz, 1 min

YEAST
White Labs WLP002 English Ale

FERMENT
20-21C/68-70F

OTHER INGREDIENTS
Demerera, cassonade or similar dark sugar, 210g/7.4oz (4.5%), added at mash stage

Brown, Belgian, bitter & strong

—

Brown ales are malty, mahogany-coloured and deep. Belgian beer is often fruity with distinctive yeast strains and a light body but high alcohol content. English bitter is easygoing and light on hops. Strong ales have heavy grain bills for high ABV and warming alcohol.

Nøgne Ø

Grimstad, Norway

#100
BARLEYWINE

▬

20 L / 5 GAL | ABV **10.1%**
OG **1.092** | FG **1.015**

The first commercial barleywine was Bass No 1 in 1903. More than 100 years later, Nøgne Ø has created its own version, and it's a worthy successor to the Burton upon Trent trailblazer. When made well barleywine stands shoulder-to-shoulder with the grand vintages of Bordeaux, but it's challenging to make. It's difficult to work with such a large volume of grist, and to get all the desired sugars out. The grain bed will be heavy, making filtering tough. If you don't hit the OG then the ABV won't be high enough and you simply won't have barleywine. This is an occasion when bumping the pre-fermentation OG up with malt extract is not a bad idea, should you need to. Other methods to ensure a strong barleywine include making two smaller worts then combining. Plus, yeast is key: without proper attenuation, you'll be left with a super-sweet and undrinkable syrup. A liquid yeast is advisable, probably two packs' worth. It's also best to rack it off the yeast after primary fermentation has finished, then again after three or four weeks, before thinking about priming and bottling. Nothing about barleywine can be rushed.

GRAIN
Maris Otter, 6.85kg/15lbs 1.6oz (88%)

Wheat malt, 800g/1lb 12.2oz (10%)

Chocolate malt, 160g/5.64oz (2%)

MASH
63C/145F for 90 mins

HOPS
Chinook, 70g/2.5oz, 90 mins

Centennial, 50g/1.8oz, 15 mins

Centennial, 50g/1.8oz, 5 mins

Columbus, 50g/1.8oz, 0 mins

Chinook, 50g/1.8oz, dry hop

YEAST
White Labs WLP007 Dry English Ale or Danstar Nottingham Ale

FERMENT
20C/68F

SPECIAL INSTRUCTIONS
This is a beer for the future. It needs long and gentle bottle ageing to reach full potential. (Even carbonation will take one or two months.) Six months' rest isn't an exaggeration; longer will be even better. Store the bottles somewhere dark and peaceful, and open one now and again to appreciate the developing characteristics

Renaissance Brewing

Blenheim, New Zealand

STONECUTTER SCOTCH ALE
SMOKED SCOTCH ALE

▬▬▬

20 L / 5 GAL | ABV **7%**
OG **1.074** | FG **1.021**

Marlborough, at the northern tip of New Zealand's South Island, is winemaking country. All that viticulture is thirsty work, but luckily the award-winning Renaissance is on hand to give those toiling farmers something decent to drink. Like many New World beers, Stonecutter takes its inspiration from a classic European style – in this case, the Scottish 'wee heavy', a strong, hearty ale originally from Edinburgh. Malts are in charge here – nine varieties provide roasty, toasty, chocolate-and-toffee complexity, and the smoked malt,

even in a tiny proportion, floats up in a delicate wisp. But this being New Zealand, locally grown hops feature too. Stonecutter is a big, big beer, and will gladly rest on wood for a while to let its flavours develop: Renaissance head brewer Andy Deuchars recommends oak chips, 15g/0.5oz, in the fermenter for three to five weeks. Put them in a sterilised bag and add to secondary, from where you can sample the beer every week or so to check how much oakiness the beer has taken on. This is a good method for those who don't have a barrel.

- -

GRAIN
Pale ale malt, 2.5kg/5lbs 8.18oz (68%)

Amber malt, 500g/1lbs 1.6oz (6.8%)

CaraAmber, 500g/1lbs 1.6oz (6.8%)

Biscuit malt, 250g/8.8oz (3.5%)

Medium crystal malt, 250g/ 8.8oz (3.5%)

Pale crystal malt, 250g/8.8oz (3.5%)

Vienna malt, 250g/8.8oz (3.5%)

Wheat malt, 250g/8.8oz (3.5%)

Smoked malt, 60g/2.1oz (0.9%)

MASH
Mash at high temperature to get the required attenuation, 68C/154.4F, 60 mins

HOPS
(60 minute boil)

Southern Cross 14% AA, 20g/ 0.7oz, first wort hops

Pacific Jade, 16g/0.6oz, hopback or whirlpool

YEAST
Wyeast 1968 London Ale

FERMENT
20C/68F

Weird Beard Brew Co

Hanwell, London, England

BORING BROWN BEER
IMPERIAL BEST BITTER

⎯⎯

20 L / 5 GAL | ABV **7.2%**
OG **1.069** | FG **1.013**

The 'boring brown beer' of the name is supposedly craft beer's absolute antithesis: interchangeably conservative beers served in pubs up and down the land, offering drinkers zero excitement and zero adventure. Weird Beard's Boring Brown Beer, however, is anything but boring. It's a range of American-style brown ales or 'imperial best bitters' featuring a single hop to impressive effect – here it's the turn of Chinook, which brings enough herbal aroma, spice and even grapefruit to stand up to the dark caramel of the Special B malt. Two malts,

one hop, loads of character – it's a simple recipe, but leaves nowhere to hide, and your brewing techniques have to be sound. Weird Beard is another inspiration for homebrewers: founders Gregg and Bryan started brewing professionally after years of amateur experimentation. Their hirsute skull logo adorns every bottle label, from the Little Things That Kill 3.8% hop-heavy session ale to the Sadako barrel-aged imperial stout. 'No gimmicks, no crap and never knowingly underhopped' is the slogan: a mantra we could all take to heart.

- -

GRAIN
Pale malt, 5.3kg/11lbs 11oz (84%)

Special B malt, 1.1kg/2lbs 6.8oz (16%)

MASH
64C/147F for 75 mins

HOPS
Chinook 13%AA, 50g/1.8oz, 60 mins

Chinook 13%AA, 20g/0.7oz, 30 mins

Chinook 13%AA, 20g/0.7oz, 15 mins

Chinook, 13%AA, 20g/0.7oz, 0 mins

YEAST
White Labs WLP007 Dry English Ale

FERMENT
19C/66F for 4 days primary, 10 days secondary

Birrificio del Ducato

Soragna, Emilia-Romagna, Italy

WINTERLUDE
TRIPEL

▬

20 L / 5 GAL | ABV **8.8%**
OG **1.079** | FG **1.012**

For a beer to be certified Trappist, it must be made by one of a select few monasteries (mostly in Belgium, although there are others in the Netherlands, Italy and even Massachussets), and all profits from sale must go to charitable causes. Tripel is a strong pale ale from the Low Countries and a classic Trappist brew: devotion to an abstemious life is not required to make or drink Del Ducato's delightful Winterlude, although with its classic European hops, Belgian yeast and candi sugar, it's faithful to the style. Kaleidoscopes of complex flavours come from these simple ingredients. Giovanni Campari's brewery, in the town of Soragna near Parma, creates beers with an elemental link to the land and heartfelt stories behind their inception: "Winterlude is a tribute to a friend who went missing, who we may meet again one day, just like the sun that is hiding behind the hill." This is a beer to age – tripels benefit from a secondary fermentation off the yeast and then a couple of months in the bottle, when it can be savoured with all the lip-smacking and pontification associated with a fine wine.

- -

GRAIN
Pilsner malt, 5.95kg/13lbs 1.9oz (86.5%)

Acidulated malt, 290g/10.2oz (4%)

Carapils, 190g/6.7oz (3%)

MASH
66C/152F for 60 mins

HOPS
Herkules, 4g/0.14oz, 70 mins

Marynka, 13g/0.45oz, 5 mins

Whitbread Goldings Variety, 25g/0.9oz, 0 mins

YEAST
Wyeast 3787 Trappist High Gravity

FERMENT
20C/68F

OTHER INGREDIENTS
White candi sugar, 450g/15.9oz (6.5%), added during the boil. Stir till it's properly dissolved to avoid it burning on the kettle

Stillwater Artisanal

Baltimore, Maryland, and Brooklyn, New York, USA

OF LOVE & REGRET
BOTANICAL FARMHOUSE ALE

━━━

20 L / 5 GAL | ABV **7%**
OG **1.058** | FG **1.004**

Of Love & Regret (also the name of the Stillwater Artisanal bar in the Brewers Hill district of Baltimore, Maryland) is described as a 'botanical farmhouse ale', and it doesn't need to be pigeonholed beyond that. From the first sip you'll realise this is no ordinary brew. Belgian beers often have spices, fruits and natural additions, and this is a particularly inventive take on that tradition. The heather, camomile, dandelion and lavender steeped in the boil add subtle garden flavours as they intertwine with the grassy, spicy Sterling and Styrian Golding: imagine a Low Countries hop field overgrown with summer wildflowers and you're somewhere near the intensely floral character of this beer. The French saison yeast brings out the herbal notes and provides the high attenutation needed for a dry finish. Aromatic malt is a speciality grain which adds a distinctive maltiness and a deep copper colour (and there's no substitute for it). These sort of open-interpretation Belgian ales really allow the imaginative brewer to become an artist. Get creative!

- -

GRAIN
Pilsner malt, 4kg/8lbs 12oz (78%)

Wheat malt, 510g/1lb 2oz (10%)

Vienna malt, 510g/1lb 2oz (10%)

Belgian aromatic malt, 100g/ 3.5oz (2%)

MASH
63C/146F for 45 mins, 75C/167F for 15 mins

HOPS
Magnum 14% AA, 7g/0.25oz, 75 mins

Sterling 7.5%, 15g/0.53oz, 10 mins

Sterling, 28g/1oz, 0 mins

Styrian Golding, 14g/0.5oz, 0 mins

YEAST
Wyeast 3711 French Saison

FERMENT
Pitch at 23C/70F then allow to rise to 24C/75F. Crash cool when activity is complete

OTHER INGREDIENTS
*Heather (Calluna vulgaris), 20g/0.7oz
Dandelion (Taraxacum officinale), 12g/0.42oz
Camomile (Matricaria chamomilla), 8g/0.28oz
Lavender (Lavandula x intermedia), 4g/0.14oz*

At flameout, steep all botanicals in a mesh bag for 10 mins

Marble Brewery

Manchester, England

MANCHESTER BITTER
BITTER

▬

20 L / 5 GAL | ABV **4.2%**
OG **1.040** | FG **1.008**

Manchester in the north of England is a proper brewing city, and Marble is Manchester through and through. It's committed to cask as well as keg and bottle, and the no-nonsense Northern branding of its logo hints at the honest and sturdily dependable beers within. Almost every style of beer has left the brewery gates, from a German latzenbier to the bourbon-barrel-aged Russian Imperial Stout, but Marble also makes the traditional sort of ales that made the city great and fuelled the Industrial Revolution in the nineteenth century. So there's the Best, English IPA, hearty Stouter Stout and Pint, an everyday bitter that really would be welcome every day. Plus the classic bitter-with-a-twist showcased here: it features the solid malt base you'd expect (Maris Otter with a smaller proportion of darker roasted crystal grains), but updates the hop bill with the Kiwi Waimea and Motueka, leaving a dry, slightly fruity and, of course, bitter finish. It's a Mancunian classic up there with the Smiths, football rivalry and rain.

- -

GRAIN
Maris Otter, 3.2kg/7lbs 0.9oz (94%)

Caramalt, 140g/4.9oz (4%)

Crystal malt 150L, 70g/2.5oz (2%)

MASH
66C/151F for 50 mins

HOPS
Herkules 16.1% AA, 3g/0.1oz, 70 mins

Goldings 3.4% AA, 20g/0.7oz, 15 mins

Waimea 18% AA, 25g/0.9oz, 0 mins (steep for 20 mins)

Motueka 8% AA, 25g/0.9oz, 0 mins (steep for 20 mins)

YEAST
Something very neutral and appropriate to the style

FERMENT
18-21C/64-70F

Rogue Ales

Newport, Oregon, USA

HAZELNUT BROWN NECTAR
AMERICAN BROWN ALE

20 L / 5 GAL | ABV **6.2%**
OG **1.057** | FG **1.016**

Nut brown ale is a traditional English-style ale, the deep burnished colour of chestnuts, with a mildly nutty taste from a complex blend of roasted malts. What it doesn't usually have is actual nuts in it, but Rogue's classic Hazelnut Brown Nectar takes things to the next level with a delicate infusion of real nut extract (Northwestern's high-quality flavourings mean the brewer can control exactly how much 'nuttiness' makes it into the beer). It also uses the Rogue strain Pacman yeast, which can be bought through Wyeast. The Oregon brewery has a history of pushing the boat out with its experimental yet always drinkable beers (Sriracha Hot stout with chilli sauce really works), but its standard range is anything but standard. Dead Guy Ale is undoubtedly the best-known heller bock in the USA (okay, probably the only known heller bock) and the Shakespeare oatmeal stout is a rated favourite the world over. Rogue also has its own farms in the Pacific Northwest growing ingredients for its brews (pumpkins, rye) as well as some that hopefully don't make it anywhere near beer (turkeys, for instance).

GRAIN
Great Western 2-row pale malt, 3.5kg/7lbs 12oz (59%)

Great Western Munich malt 10L, 0.9kg/2lbs (15%)

Great Western Crystal malt 75L, 680g/1lb 8oz (11%)

Baird Brown malt, 312g/11oz (5%)

Great Western Crystal malt 15L, 255g/9oz (4%)

Great Western Crystal malt 120L, 255g/9oz (4%)

Franco-Belges Kiln Coffee malt, 113g/4oz (2%)

MASH
67C/152F for 60 mins

HOPS
(70 minute boil)

Perle pellets 9% AA, 17g/0.6oz, 60 mins

Sterling pellets 5%AA, 14g/0.5oz, 0 mins (ten-minute hop stand)

YEAST
Wyeast 1764 Pacman

FERMENT
16-18C/60-65F

OTHER INGREDIENTS
Northwestern hazelnut extract, ½ tsp, to be added at bottling stage

Williams Bros Brewing Co

Alloa, Scotland

80/-
SCOTTISH ALE

▬▬▬

20 L / 5 GAL | ABV **4.2%**
OG **1.043** | FG **1.012**

Scotch ale is known to most people worldwide as something strong, sweet-ish and richly mahogany in colour. It often has an embarrassing name like 'Big Tam's Kilt Lifter'. It's not, unsurprisingly, what most Scots drink day-to-day. A more appropriate contender for a national pint would be 80 shilling (called '80 bob' or even just '80' by locals – it's named after an old system of taxation on a barrel, whereby the strongest and best-quality beer commanded keener interest from the exciseman). Scott and Bruce Williams, based in the historical Central Belt brewing hub of Alloa, have done more than anyone to revive and maintain ancient Scottish styles; as well as their Fraoch heather ale, a resurrection of a beer that predated hop use by a good few centuries, is this updated 80/-. Its generous malts and English bittering hops are faithful to a traditional version, but then the Northwestern US aroma hops and orange peel infusion give it a modern flourish (although those ingredients still tread quietly – this is a malty beer). Drink with a *slainte* (Gaelic for cheers).

GRAIN
Pale malt, 2.87kg/6lbs 5oz (75%)

Wheat malt, 380g/13.4oz (10%)

Crystal malt 115L, 250g/8.8oz (6.5%)

Chocolate malt, 170g/6oz (4.5%)

Milled oats, 150g/5.3oz (4%)

MASH
70C/158F for 50 mins

HOPS
First Gold, 14.5g/0.5oz, 60 mins

Savinski Goldings, 11g/0.4oz, 45 mins

Amarillo, 10g/0.35oz, 0 mins

Cascade, 10g/0.35oz, dry hop

YEAST
White Labs WLP039 Nottingham Ale

FERMENT
20C/68F

OTHER INGREDIENTS
Sweet orange peel, 40g/1.4oz, boil for 15 mins

	DEN TOWN	HELLS LAGER	4.6% £4.
	PIVO 12°		5% £5.0
	MDEN TOWN	PALE ALE	4.0% £4.5
KEG	BEAVERTOWN	GAMMA RAY	5.4% £5.0
KEG	TO ØL	GARDEN OF EDEN	6.4% £6.
KEG	WEIHENSTEPHANER	HEFEWEISSBIER	5.4% £5.
KEG	ANCHOR	SPRING ALE	7.2% £6.
KEG	CAMDEN TOWN	INK STOUT	4.4% £4.
KEG	MIKKELLER	IT'S ALIVE	8% £3
KEG	TROUBADOUR	IMPERIAL STOUT	9% £

OLIVER'S CIDER AND PERRY MEET

NT	KEG	TROUBADOUR	WESTKUST		
NT	KEG	LERVIG	KONRAD'S STOUT		
NT	KEG	FOUNDERS	CURMUDGEON	9.8%	
PINT	CASK	DARK STAR	HOPHEAD	3.8%	£3.80 PINT
PINT	CASK	WILD BEER	BIBBLE	4.2%	£3.90 PINT
NT	CASK	BAD	WILD GRAVITY	5.2%	£4.20 PINT
PINT	CASK				PINT
NT	CIDER	LILLEY'S	STARGAZER CIDER	4.5%	£4.20 PINT
ALF	CIDER	BARBOURNE	STRAWBERRY CIDER	4%	£4.40 PINT
HALF	CIDER	OLIVER'S	DRY CIDER	6%	£4.40 PINT

AKER & TAP TAKEOVER ON THURSDAY JUNE 18TH

Glossary

—

As befits a centuries-old practice, brewing comes with its own often pleasingly medieval-sounding vocabulary, many of it borrowed from German and Old English, including the witchy-sounding 'wort' (properly pronounced 'wert', if you're being pedantic), and 'copper', a traditional name for the boil kettle.

ADJUNCTS
Unmalted grains added to a mash;
sometimes other additions too (spices
or flavourings).

ALPHA ACIDS (AA)
Acids in hops which contribute towards
the overall bitterness of the beer.

AERATING
Oxygenating boiled wort to allow yeast
to thrive.

AROMA HOPS
Hops added after the first half-hour or so
of the boil: they are usually low in alpha
acids and provide aroma.

ATTENUATION
Conversion of sugar to CO_2 and alcohol
(by yeast).

BITTERING HOPS
Hops added at the start of the boil:
after an hour of boiling they give up their
desired bitter flavours.

BOILING
The process of infusing wort with the
bitterness, flavour and aroma of hops.
Done in a boil kettle, aka a copper.

BOTTLING/KEGGING
Transferring beer to a receptacle suitable
for convenient consumption.

CONDITIONING
Resting beer in a bottle, barrel, cask or
keg to allow it to carbonate and develop
in flavour.

FERMENTING
The process by which yeast converts
fermentable sugars into alcohol and CO_2.

FINING
A substance added during the brewing
process to clarify the beer (Protofloc or
Irish moss).

FLAMEOUT
Literally, the moment when the heat under
the boil is extinguished: also refers to
the moment when hops are added to the
wort to impart maximum aroma. See also
whirlpool.

FLOCCULATION
The act of clustering or clumping
together, in the case of brewing, yeast
solids in the fermenter.

GRAVITY, SPECIFIC
The density of liquid (in brewing, the
concentration of sugar in liquid).

GRIST
Ground grain for mashing.

KRAUSEN
A foam of proteins and yeast that forms
on the wort during primary fermentation.
Looks disturbing, is actually a reassuring
sign that all is going well.

LAUTERING

The process of rinsing the grains of all their fermentable sugars and taking the wort to a pre-boil volume. It involves two stages: recirculation (aka vorlauf), using the existing water in the tun, and sparging: sprinkling fresh water over the grain bed.

LIQUOR

Water used directly in a brew. The total volume needed is split into strike water (used to mash) and sparge water (in the sparging process).

MASH HOPS

Hops added in the mash for bittering. An uncommon practice.

MASHING

The process of soaking grains and adjuncts in hot water in the mash tun to extract sugars. Can be done at one temperature (single-rest) or variable-temperature stages (multi-rest). Mashing out is the process of raising the temperature sharply at the end of the infusion to halt enzyme action.

PITCHING

Adding yeast to wort.

PRIMING

Adding sugar (or malt extract, or occasionally yeast) to wort before bottling to facilitate the creation of carbonation in the bottle.

RACKING

Transferring wort from one vessel to another, typically from a primary fermenter to a second, or from a fermenter to a priming vessel.

TRUB

Unwanted sediment in the boil kettle and fermenter, consisting mainly of hop matter, proteins and dead yeast cells.

WHIRLPOOL

When brewers spin the post-boil wort at high speed to form a mound of undesirable solids in the middle. 'Whirlpool hops' are sometimes added at this stage.

WORT

Sweet liquid taken from the tun after the mash, containing fermentable sugars.

Index

—

H

Acknowledgements

—

Firstly, a huge thanks to my brilliant commissioning editor Zena, who made this book a hundred times better in every way. Thanks to Ashleigh for her amazing illustrations and book design, and to Charlie for his great photographs. Also, the technical expertise of Talfryn Provis-Evans was indispensable.

Thanks to all the breweries that I cajoled, encouraged and hassled to share their recipes with me. They're all world-beating, but for extra distinction, special mention to James at Brewdog, Evin at The Kernel, Logan, Jenn and Nick at Beavertown, Vinnie at Russian River, John at Brouwerij de Molen, Henok at Omnipollo, Brian at Stillwater Artisanal, Jayne and Danielle at Two Birds, Tony at Boneyard, Chris Pilkington at Põhjala, Chad at Crooked Stave, Scott Williams at Williams Bros, Doug Odell, Stu at Yeastie Boys and all the NZ Craft Beer Collective, Fabio at Baladin, Andrew Bell and Benjamin Weiss at Bruery Terreux, and Ben Love at Gigantic.

Thanks to everyone who helped me assemble an incredible collection of beers from around the world to take pictures of: Splandos, Rob, Tina, Benjamin, Ben, Fabio, Chris, and Jules at Hop Hideout. And for allowing me to invade their premises and turn them into photographic studios: everyone at the Kings Arms, Bethnal Green, the Three Johns, Islington, and Ubrew, Bermondsey.

Big thanks to Will and Tom at Clapton Craft, the best craft beer shop in the world!

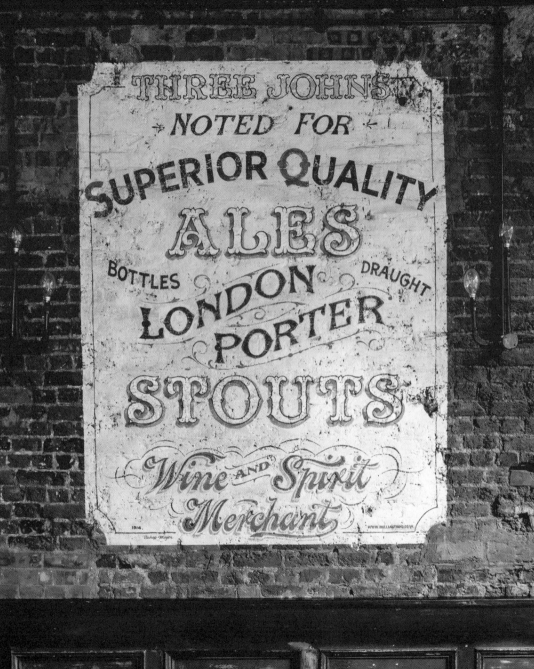